Self-Representation and Digital Culture

Self-Representation and Digital Culture

Nancy Thumim
University of Leeds, UK

First published 2012 by
PALGRAVE MACMILLAN

Palgrave Macmillan in the UK is an imprint of Macmillan Publishers Limited,
registered in England, company number 785998, of Houndmills, Basingstoke,
Hampshire RG21 6XS.

Palgrave Macmillan in the US is a division of St Martin's Press LLC,
175 Fifth Avenue, New York, NY 10010.

Palgrave Macmillan is the global academic imprint of the above companies
and has companies and representatives throughout the world.

Palgrave® and Macmillan® are registered trademarks in the United States,
the United Kingdom, Europe and other countries.

ISBN 978–0–230–22966–2

This book is printed on paper suitable for recycling and made from fully
managed and sustained forest sources. Logging, pulping and manufacturing
processes are expected to conform to the environmental regulations of the
country of origin.

A catalogue record for this book is available from the British Library.

A catalog record for this book is available from the Library of Congress.

10   9   8   7   6   5   4   3   2   1
21 20 19 18 17 16 15 14 13 12

Printed and bound in the United States of America
by Edwards Brothers Malloy, Inc.

For Jesse Elvis Thumim Blake, born in the middle
of it all, 2010

Contents

Acknowledgements

I have benefited hugely from the insightful comments of colleagues in several institutions. At the London School of Economics, I am grateful to my PhD supervisor, Sonia Livingstone, and to Roger Silverstone, Lilie Chouliaraki, Nick Couldry, Zoe Sujon and Giota Alevizou for comments (and sometimes collaborations) at crucial stages. I am grateful to colleagues in the Mediatized Stories Network, in particular Knut Lundby. This network introduced me to Gunn Sara Enli, with whom I developed ideas about how her work on socialising intersected with my ideas about self-representation. At Goldsmiths, Bev Skeggs and Helen Wood got me thinking about my ideas on self-representation in relation to reality TV.

My new academic home, the Institute of Communications Studies at the University of Leeds, has provided a stimulating environment for finishing the book. In particular, Stephen Coleman has been a thoughtful, critical and supportive reader, and the Leeds Media Ecology project team (Stephen Coleman, Giles Moss, Jay G. Blumler, Judith Stamper and Steven McDermott) has provided stimulating debate that has helped to sharpen the focus of the final manuscript. The book has also benefited enormously from the thoughtful comments of two anonymous reviewers. I am grateful to the Economic and Social Research Council and the Research Council of Norway for funding that allowed me to pursue this research. I have also enjoyed working with Felicity Plester, my helpful editor at Palgrave Macmillan.

Ordinary people participating in the *Capture Wales, London's Voices* and *Ethical Scenarios of Class and Self* research projects helped to make this book. Producers, curators and other staff at the Museum of London and BBC Wales New Media Department, as well as representatives of funding bodies and partner organisations who spoke with me and let me observe their activities, also helped to make this book. Mandy Rose, in particular, tipped me off about an innovative new project at BBC Wales and became a good friend over time. The practical help of Vanessa Cragoe over a number of years and Divya

Maharajh at a crucial moment most recently has been invaluable. Then, of course, I am grateful to all the people who have been with me along the way, especially Ella Thumim, Rebecca Geldard, Molly Conisbee, Hannah Griffiths, Brand Thumim, Linda Barr, Eleanor Barr, Joshua Thumim, Anna Jephcote, Luca and Maeve Thumim. Gary Blake, Rhiannon Blake and Jesse Elvis Thumim Blake slowed me down and showed me the view – and it's a better book for it. Finally, Janet Thumim gave me a taste for the politics of representation and has consistently and constantly helped me pursue it, sometimes as a mother, sometimes as a scholarly and critical reader, and always as a taliswoman.

Nancy Thumim
Leeds, January 2012

1
Introduction: Self-Representation and Digital Culture

Self-representation

This book addresses the phenomenal proliferation of self-representation by so-called 'ordinary people' in contemporary digital culture, offering the reader a way of making sense of diverse examples of what I ultimately suggest should now be understood as a genre in its own right. The 'call' for participation via self-representation extends from *invitations* by publicly funded bodies (see Chapter 4, 'Broadcasters', and Chapter 5, 'Museum and Art Worlds') to those from private companies, such as TV companies and channels (see Chapter 4, 'Broadcasters'), to the self-motivated practice of social networking (see Chapter 6, 'Self-Representation Online'). This volume specifically focuses on the questions arising from the proliferation of self-representation by 'ordinary people' across a range of sites, but we should note that self-representation is phenomenal and therefore precisely is not limited to the practices of one group of people or another; it is not only amateurs who produce representations of themselves as 'ordinary' but also professional creative practitioners, such as fine artists and documentarists, who contribute to this genre (Dovey and Rose, forthcoming; Renov, 2004). Opportunities for self-representation are also a usual part of the activities of various kinds of organisation whose key purpose is not cultural, from corporations to pressure groups. Four examples illustrate the ubiquity of opportunities for self-representation.

Firstly note the use of an opportunity for self-representation in BP's corporate sponsorship of the London Olympics 2012; the

1

corporation currently most well-known for the Gulf of Mexico oil spill in 2011 is 'the official Oil and Gas Partner for the London 2012 Games'. BP's involvement in the Games includes enabling 'creative participation' by young people in partnership with cultural institutions such as the Tate, Aardman Animation and the British Museum:

> As part of the Cultural Olympiad, BP's arts and cultural partners are putting together extraordinary programmes and events for young people, to get them involved and to be more creative.
>
> (BP website, July 2011)

Secondly consider an electronic games company. Nintendo has a web page which elicits and claims to display customers' personal to-camera video stories of identity coupled with Nintendo game playing. Self-representation of ordinary, everyday life works here to promote the Nintendo brand and products:

> Why do you play? Promoting maths at school; exercising to get in shape after childbirth; overcoming personal fears or even finding a way to pass the time. We have captured some of these moments for you on our Nintendo Stories website. Now it's your turn to share your personal Nintendo Story with us!
>
> (Nintendo website, July 2011)

Thirdly note the use of self-representations as a normal part of the work carried out by contemporary campaigning groups, such as Asthma UK's current 'Get it off your chest' campaign:

> Let's get asthma taken seriously! Help us to ensure asthma is not forgotten amongst the proposed changes to our healthcare system. We want to make sure asthma is seen as a priority, show the importance of improving care and for everyone to realise just how serious it can be. So start sharing your: angry stories, sad stories, frustrating stories, surprising stories, happy stories. Or add your voice to the map by showing your support.
>
> (Asthma UK website, July 2011)

Finally consider the diverse kinds of space that members of the public routinely occupy: doctor's surgeries, dental practices, hospitals, schools, supermarkets, nurseries, restaurants, shopping centres and railway stations. I suggest that in any of these it is not uncommon to encounter invitations to 'tell your story', 'have your say' and otherwise submit or display (in various textual forms) what is effectively a representation of oneself.

The existence of a diverse range of sites offering what looks like self-representation calls for their critical analysis. Self-representations are not all the same kind of thing and they are not all serving the same kind of purpose. Self-representations do not all construct the 'ordinary people' they feature in the same way and they do not all take the same textual form. They do not all use digital technology in the same way, if they use it at all, but they *do* all exist in the digital culture. This book aims to bring together a range of examples of self-representation, in order to explore the meanings of a contemporary phenomenon that is intimately entwined with digital culture. In the following chapters I use the concept of *mediation process* (discussed in Chapter 3) as a way to differentiate between representations that differ in terms of both form and politics. By means of a discussion of varied examples I shall establish that we now need to think in terms of a *genre* of self-representation (discussed in Chapter 7). It follows from this that there are generic conventions being used *across* our digital culture. There are also, we should note, practices of self-representation which challenge the norms and conventions that have become established as a genre – play with the genre of self-representation is to be found across digital culture in YouTube videos and on TV. No matter how playful or how conventional, self-representations are always, necessarily, mediated. In this book I offer an approach for exploring the question of how self-representations are mediated – one that can be used to explore what diverse examples of the genre mean.

The mediation of self-representation is both a political and a cultural matter because of the range of associations that we make. By political I mean to invoke political with a small 'p' (the political dimension that arguably shapes most, if not all, interactions in everyday life) and political with a capital 'P' (the institutions of democratic representation). Here I follow Chantal Mouffe's distinction between what she terms 'politics and the political' (Mouffe, 2005):

> this is how I distinguish between 'the political' and 'politics': by 'the political' I mean the dimension of antagonism which I take to be constitutive of human societies, while by 'politics' I mean the set of practices and institutions through which an order is created, organizing human coexistence in the context of conflictuality provided by the political.
>
> (2005, p. 9)

On thinking of self-representation, the range of associations that we make include (but are by no means limited to) the democratic connotations consequent upon the self speaking on behalf of itself (see also Morley, 2006, for a discussion of the political). The idea is raised that the self can impact on formal political procedure, thus 'politics' (in Mouffe's terms) are invoked by the very idea of self-representation. 'The political' (in Mouffe's terms) is invoked both because self-representations promise to deliver authentic accounts of individual 'ordinary people' and because they promise to provide therapeutic benefits to individuals. Authenticity and therapy are 'political' with a small 'p' because the meanings of authenticity and the benefits of therapy take shape within human relations structured by race, gender, class, sexuality, age, nationality and other factors. Importantly, the range of associations that are raised by the idea of self-representation are not all provoked by every self-representation. Analysis of the processes of mediation helps us unpack the imagined and actual differences between – for example, the self-representation that is made as part of a community-oriented project and the self-representation that is consequent upon appearing in a reality TV programme. Moreover the focus on mediation shows how we can be alert to the ways in which this range of self-representations is both produced by and productive of our digital culture.

Digital technologies have broadened, beyond recognition, the possibilities for mediated interpersonal communication. One-to-one and one-to-many communication is now both technically possible and variously taken up – as scholarship in this area since the 1990s has explored (e.g. Lievrouw and Livingstone, 2002; Lister et al., 2003;

Rheingold, 1993; Turkle, 1997). But Lister et al. emphasise a key distinction between the Internet and the subsequent development of the World Wide Web in terms of the participating audience or user:

> Fundamentally, the text-based Internet required writing (sending) and reading (interpretation) for the user to function. The web requires 'clicking', selecting from graphic menus, reading, and further selecting.
>
> (2003, p. 182)

Writing in 2003, Lister et al. observe increased participation on the internet; while they ascribe it to commercial developments, they conclude that internet communication is best understood through a framework of active audiences:

> Our contention is that the web has made the Internet a fundamentally less interactive space and that this shift in the character of the Internet necessitates a shift in analytic methodology that is more in line with ways of thinking about active audiences seeking participatory spaces in mediated culture rather than transformative new patterns of human communication and subjectivity.
>
> (2003, p. 182)

Participatory spaces online – or online 'communities' as they are often referred to – should be understood as part of ongoing struggles to makes spaces for more democratic media production. The history of these struggles is discussed in Chapter 2.

Ubiquitous self-representations may look alike but analysis of the various dimensions of mediation process shaping their production and display highlights the important distinctions between them. For example, in the following chapters we will see that attempts to democratise media production have often turned to facilitating self-representation as a strategy for increasing participation and hence, it is thought, securing enhanced democracy. Meanwhile in many online socialising networks the representation of the self is a condition of participation. The three key dimensions of mediation processes are elaborated in Chapter 3.

Conceptualising self-representation

I first came across the term 'self-representation' during the 1990s when interviewing Bob Long, Chris Mohr and Mandy Rose, then the producers of the TV series *Video Nation*, at the Community Programme Unit at the BBC. Self-representation was a rather matter of fact description used to explain the kinds of project carried out within the Access tradition at the Community Programme Unit. Clearly this idea has all sorts of practical histories in, for example, Access TV, community and activist video art practices, and *Mass Observation* (I consider this history in Chapter 2).[1] Today, rather than being a minority activity, the increasing appearance of what look like opportunities for self-representation across media and cultural spaces is accompanied by scholarship attending to this practice. Thus the term 'self-representation' is now regularly used to refer to activities of participating audiences in digital culture, alongside other, related, terms like performance of self and presentation of self (e.g. Cheung, 2000; Livingstone, 2008; Yee and Bailenson, 2007), and, most recently, self-revelation (Ellis, 2012). I suggest that the term 'self-representation' should be considered as distinct from notions of either presentation or performance of self.

Research has drawn on Goffman's (1959) work on the presentation of self to problematise the distinction between online and offline selves (e.g. Livingstone, 2008). However, the porosity of these 'borders' does not remove the requirement to address circulating symbolic forms, that is, representations. When someone produces a self-representation they produce a bounded text, however fleeting and ephemeral that text might be. The idea of self-representation is different to that of 'performance of self' since, as work on performance of self suggests, we all 'perform the self' all of the time and this is neither a bounded nor indeed a necessarily conscious process (e.g. Abercrombie and Longhurst, 1998; Butler, 1990). Self-representation and the concept of representation in itself do not replace performance or presentation, but are conceptually different. Performances of self, presentations of self and self-representations coexist and, of course, all are subject to processes of mediation. However the precise notion of the *representation* raises questions about the *mediation of a textual object*. In this view, when a self-representation is produced it becomes a text that has the potential for subsequent engagement. I suggest we revisit theories of representation in order to move beyond using the term 'self-representation' as if its meaning is clear and commonsensical, and specifically in order to understand the digital culture in which self-representations appear to have become so prevalent.

The practice of self-representation did not begin with modern media and communication systems. Theorisation of the representation of the self has a history in scholarship as long as the history of the idea of the self. The concept of the self must begin with the modern notion of the subject, which can be traced to the seventeenth-century post-Renaissance period as John Berger notes in his 1967 essay, 'The Moment of Cubism':

> The Copernican revolution, Protestantism, the Counter-Reformation destroyed the Renaissance position. With this destruction modern subjectivity was born.
>
> (1967, p. 82)

This summary of a wide set of historical processes brings us to the birth of the self, and individual selves became, from then on, subject(s) of representation.

In a discussion of factual representation in TV, John Corner highlights the crucial point that representation must always involve choices:

> Out of the range of possible kinds of reality open to documentary treatment, a topic is chosen as the subject of a film or programme. But how will this topic be depicted in particular images and sounds? The initial decision here concerns what to film, whom to film and what kinds of sound (including speech) to record. No matter whether the topic is an abstract one (for example, loneliness in student communities) or a physically grounded one (for example, the problem of heavy traffic in rural areas), *a strategy of representation and of visualisation* is required.
>
> (1995a, p. 79) (Italics in original)

The point I want to draw out here is that representations are made by one set of people (in this case film-makers) of another (subjects).

As Tessa Perkins has persuasively argued, the academic study of representation remains theoretically and politically important, just as it becomes difficult to justify in the context of post-structuralism. The study of representation is, she held, fundamental simply because representations are always political:

> films, *along with other forms of representation*, play an important role in forming ideas about, and attitudes to, the world, in alleviating anxiety and even in diffusing conflict – in short, they do do political work.
>
> (Perkins, 2000, p. 76) (Italics in original)

The concept of *self-representation* contains an even more explicitly political claim than *representation* and this is because the term itself contains a challenge to the idea that it is the job of one set of people to represent another set of people. This challenge is present in the implicit (and sometimes explicit) claim that in self-representation people are *'doing it for themselves'*. And it is precisely because of this claim that Corner's earlier notion of a 'strategy of representation' urgently needs revisiting. In instances of self-representation there must still (always) be choices about *which* aspects of self to represent and *how* to represent them, in other words 'strategies of representation and of visualisation' (Corner, 1995a). Moreover, because self-representations must, by definition, be mediated, the challenge that is connoted by the claim that someone is 'doing it for themselves' does not turn out to be at all straightforward – self-representations, to borrow Perkin's phrase, 'do do political work' (Perkins, 2000).

As Graham Murdock noted over ten years ago, the term 'self-representation' invokes both democratic and cultural representation, brought together via the notion of cultural citizenship (Murdock, 1999). Murdock observes that, in the historical development of citizen rights,

> it was clear that, in addition to guaranteeing basic material conditions for participation, full citizenship also required access to relevant symbolic resources and the competences to use them effectively.
>
> (1999, p. 11)

However the term 'self-representation' also privileges the *experience* of the individual self. Eva Illouz argues that the notion of a self as construed in therapeutic discourse became institutionalised, fundamentally shaping modern American capitalist society via three key movements – the adoption of this discourse by the American state, by second-wave feminists and by Vietnam veterans (Illouz, 2007, pp. 57–62). Suggesting that the state and two civil groups were all key in valorising the public sharing of the self and its emotional experience via the therapeutic narrative, Illouz develops the notion of 'emotional capitalism'. Illouz's analysis suggests that individual emotional *experience* is fundamental to any kind of modern self-representation.[2] The concept and discourse of self-representation contains a valorisation of experience which has a therapeutic function and at the same time invokes the possibility of material political outcomes, which has a democratic function. Thus the very words, 'idea' and 'practice' of self-representation hold together two (uncomfortably different) discourses – that is, to say therapy, with its emphasis on individual, personal and even private development, and democracy, in which the aggregation of individuals as the collective public is privileged.

Murdock has discussed the tension between experience as 'ordinariness' and experience as democratic voice in relation to TV (see the discussion of broadcasters in Chapter 4). This tension is further captured in the debate between Emmanuel Schegloff and Michael Billig. Schegloff claimed that ordinariness emphasises the commonality and shared positions from which we all speak, while Billig argued that 'the ordinary' works to deny difference and the unequal power relations to which it must give rise (Billig, 1999; Schegloff, 1999). The debate is important because it sheds light on what Marjorie Mayo has described as the 'return of community', through which self-representation becomes tightly articulated with a governmental emphasis on locally based 'community' initiatives across areas such as cultural policy or neighbourhood regeneration (Mayo, 2006).[3]

In the museum sector, for example, discourses of community are visible in institutional strategies for participation, which frequently include forms of self-representation. In this way museum practices are situated in a field of ambivalence via the discourse of self-representation – alongside many contemporary institutions.[4] It therefore seems timely to explore how contemporary practices of self-representation, situated as they often are in discourses of ordinariness, or community, or both, might enable or hinder the democratic function of public participation and to ask what else self-representation *does*. If we accept a) that self-representations are proliferating in digital culture and b) that the concept of self-representation always invokes two particular discourses (therapeutic and democratic), then it becomes urgent to explore how self-representations (in all their diversity) are mediated in digital culture. This discussion begins to suggest that the very processes by which mediation shapes self-representation are of the utmost importance. It is precisely through particular processes of mediation that self-representations come to be shaped in certain kinds of way and not others; according to, for example, power relations within and across institutions, technological capabilities and cultural expectations, as addressed in Chapter 3.

Digital culture

Digital culture and its variations has become a widely used label for diverse scholarship relating to new media and society (e.g. Coleman, forthcoming; Deuze, 2006; Silver, 2004). David Silver notes the overlapping labels describing work contributing to 'internet studies':

> For the time being, it appears as though the largest umbrella underneath which many of us would huddle is called internet studies. While simultaneously drawing and building from other, older research streams (computers and composition, computer-supported cooperative work, hyper/cybertext theory, and human–computer interaction, to name just a few) and waiting for others to join, follow, or contest – internet studies (also labelled studies of cyberculture, digital culture, information society, or new media) continues to grow as what can only be called a meta-field of study.
>
> (2004, p. 55)

Even more than 'cyberculture', 'information society' or 'new media', the term 'digital culture' indicates a focus on culture at the broadest level; this term implies that the affordances and the constraints resulting from digital technologies shape everyday life across its multiple facets, for everyone, just as electricity and print were seen as doing in previous eras. Moreover, today's hype about technology is

hype about digital technology and the hype matters – hype is akin
to myth, in Vincent Mosco's argument, and many of today's myths
concern the digital:

> A myth is alive if it continues to give meaning to human life, if it
> continues to represent some important part of the collective men-
> tality of a given age, and if it continues to render socially and
> intellectually tolerable what would otherwise be experienced as
> incoherence.
>
> (2005, p. 29)

My interviews with and observations of people who took part in
projects to make and display their own self-representations suggest
that widespread belief in the idea that a self-representation displayed
on a digital platform will be 'there' forever provokes a range of
responses from delight to disinterest to dismay. This is just one example of how feelings about the digital play a part in the processes of
mediation shaping contemporary self-representations. There is a long
history to what Leo Marx termed the 'technological sublime' (Marx,
1964). Sometimes fears and desires about technology very closely
echo those that went before – electricity in the nineteenth century,
and print before it, were both transformative in tangible, everyday
ways as well as being the subject of fear and desire (e.g. Carey, 1992;
Marx, 1964; Nye, 1992). But ideas about the digital are also specific
to this particular technology and the culture it both produces and
is produced by. In this book I keep the context of the imaginary in
mind, while looking at specific examples of self-representation in digital culture. The major obstacle in this discussion is that we are in the
process of the transformations – both real and imagined – associated
with digital technology right now and do not, therefore, have the
benefit of hindsight to pick apart the real and the imagined. I am,
clearly, writing both from within, and about, digital culture.

Thus in deploying the term 'digital culture' I mean to invoke
both the tangible and the amorphous implications of digital technology. Stephen Coleman and Karen Ross (focusing on the internet)
summarise the range of tangible implications:

> Like broadcasting in the early twentieth century and the printing
> press five hundred years earlier, the Internet has brought about
> new ways of producing, acquiring, sharing and challenging what

people need to know. It has changed the ways in which older media are used. It has reshaped wider social relations, often having unintended consequences for key social activities such as working, learning, travelling, purchasing goods, making friends and being governed.

(2010, pp. 34–5)

Accompanying these wide-ranging aspects of digital culture are the various, sometimes imperceptible, ways in which living in the age of digital technology shapes everyday culture. Seen in this light, the ascription *digital culture* includes the very many cases where digital technology is *not* accessed and used. Coleman and Ross draw on Manuel Castells to emphasise this point:

> If the Internet is significant in cultural, economic and political terms, we must also take account of Castells' (2001) claim that 'exclusion from these networks is one of the most damaging forms of exclusion in our economy and in our culture.'
>
> (2010, pp. 29–30)

Moreover, digital technology includes, but is not limited to, the internet, shaping production and consumption of images, texts and sounds across culture, as many scholars have pointed out. This is not to suggest that, for example, a pencil drawing on a piece of paper no longer occurs, but rather to point out that such a drawing can potentially be scanned and circulated via digital technology – with all that that implies. In his book *Beyond Technology: Children's Learning in the Age of Digital Culture*, David Buckingham insists on this cultural and social construction of the meaning of technology:

> I continue to regard these things as *media* rather than as *technologies*. I see them as ways of representing the world, and of communicating – and I seek to understand these phenomena as social and cultural processes, rather than primarily as technical ones.
>
> (2007, p. viii) (Italics in original)

The term 'digital culture' suggests an understanding of 'culture' and 'cultural processes', as Buckingham puts it here, at the very broadest of levels; of course, within this definition of digital culture we can point to myriad digital *cultures*. This book addresses the interaction between self-representation and digital culture, understanding culture at this broadest level. I hope that the ideas presented here will provoke thinking about the interaction between self-representation and digital culture in digital cultures beyond those examples explored in the following pages. I want to make two assertions at the start of this book. One, I suggest that to approach digital culture as a set of cultural, social and political processes, we require the analytical concept of mediation – a concept and a theoretical orientation which I discuss in Chapter 3. The second assertion I want to make is that self-representation and digital culture are now inextricably linked, thus one facet of digital culture requiring theorisation is precisely the ubiquitous genre of self-representation.

Theoretical approach

The theoretical approach of this book is rooted in studies of the audience and, in particular, in Stuart Hall's encoding/decoding model and subsequent notions of a circuit of culture (e.g. Hall, 1973, 1997). The makers of self-representations in today's digital culture are members of the audience or, as Jay Rosen (2006) has argued, they are 'the people formerly known as the audience'. In the following chapter I explore the long history of audiences appearing as part of media representations – a history that is properly a part of audience studies. Hall, and Hall's later work with Du Gay et al., insists that we understand meaning-making as a process and that we aim to take into account different positions in these circular processes in order to understand how meaning is produced. This means, to put it crudely, taking production, text and reception into account. Hall's earlier model always put into question the possibility of clear distinctions between these sites and more recently it has become commonplace to suggest that in digital culture analytic boundaries between production, text and reception are increasingly difficult to sustain. I suggest specifically that, as audiences produce self-representations as a more and more everyday activity, this is absolutely the case. Understanding self-representation, then, requires us to use concepts emphasising the sense of process and movement between sites of production, text and reception. Thus in order to explore self-representation in digital culture I deploy the notion of mediation process (e.g. Silverstone, 1999, 2005) which I understand as emerging from the theorising of these earlier ideas about audiences.

In this book I explore some exemplary cases of mediated self-representation – the concept of mediation is discussed in detail in Chapter 3. In considering cases of mediated self-representation I look at production, text and participation. The material referred to in this book was collected between 2003 and 2010 and there is a particular emphasis on two UK-based publicly funded projects – *London's Voices* at the Museum of London and *Capture Wales* at BBC Wales – where extensive in-depth qualitative research raised the questions and provoked the theoretical account of self-representation in global digital culture, which is proposed and argued through this book.[5] The UK interview excerpts are from interviews conducted between 2003 and 2005. Further examples of self-representation in digital culture are considered including the Smithsonian Institute in Washington DC, USA, reality TV programming in the UK, Knowle West Media Centre and Arnolfini in Bristol, UK, and the American-based, but internationally used, social networking site Facebook.[6] The methodological approach of the book is qualitative in a general sense. I draw on in-depth interviews, focus groups and observations with employees of media and cultural institutions whose work focuses on the facilitation of self-representation, and with members of the public who are producers of self-representations. I also draw on analysis of institutional documents, both internal and publicly available on the Institutions' websites (as well as the websites themselves). Lastly I consider the textual self-representations that are emergent through processes of mediation.

Although work on texts has been criticised in media studies, partly because audience research has made clear that people understand texts in widely diverse ways, textual analysis has certain advantages when the interest is in exploring how social tensions and ambivalences are played out at the level of language and visual meaning (see, e.g., Chouliaraki, 2006; Fairclough, 1995; Macdonald, 2003). In this book textual analysis is used to identify the tensions in meaning surrounding self-representation in institutional and 'everyday' discourses and, thereby, the competing definitions of public implied in the practice of self-representation. Visual and discursive analysis reveals *how* discursive tensions ultimately produce certain meanings about self-representation as dominant thereby legitimising certain definitions of the public. Detailed analysis of the texts of self-representation enables us to speculate about the meanings and conflicts about meaning that they and their display generate. If we take the idea that texts do political work seriously (Perkins, 2000), then we must encounter and make sense of texts that lie very far outside any kind of canon – like the self-representations of ordinary people.

In the spirit of Adam Jaworski and Hywel Bishop's study of nation-building as a discursive practice of the imagination (Jaworski and Bishop, 2003), this book explores a range of domains to ask 'what discursive and visual practices have been mobilized to construct common sense perspectives' (Jaworski and Bishop, 2003), which position ordinary people in relation to the sites where they practise self-representation (museums, cultural institutions, entertainment TV, social networking)? I ask how the practice of audiencehood as a participatory, self-representational activity is normalised (through the textual spaces for self-representation, through policy documents, through publicity materials) in digital culture – and with what outcomes of meaning.

In order to make a general analysis of proliferating self-representations in unlike spaces, the empirical data in what follows are necessarily heterogeneous. Across this varied data there are inevitably differences in form, content and rhetorical goals, and yet the data coalesce to produce the 'common sense' with which this book is concerned. This is the common sense that results in the establishment of a genre of self-representation available as a common cultural resource to be *used* in various and indeed contradictory ways (such as in discourses of therapy and democracy, as noted above).

Chapter layout and rationale

The book is organised in seven chapters. Chapter 2 explores the history of representing ordinary people in media and cultural spaces. I begin with a discussion of the contested, and arguably over-used, concepts 'ordinary people' and 'community' that are so central to the historical and contemporary representation of members of the public. The chapter then moves from the period of the late eighteenth and early nineteenth centuries to the present day. Firstly I explore the late eighteenth- and early nineteenth-century construction and representation of publics as part of nations. The next part considers a period beginning in the early twentieth century, when ideas about who constituted the public were fought over and expanded. Following this, I look at the mid- and late twentieth century, when the limitations of the nation as a reference point for representing who ordinary people are become sharply highlighted. In the next part I explore the contemporary scene and note an emphasis on ordinary people representing themselves in media and cultural spaces. The chapter ends with the proposition that the phenomenon of ubiquitous self-representation presents problems of meaning that are social, cultural and political, and that are best approached with the concept of mediation processes.

In Chapter 3 this book's primary theoretical concept of mediation process is elaborated. I suggest that the concept provides an enabling orientation both to the contemporary media and cultural landscape, and to debates in the fields of media, communication, film and cultural studies. The chapter begins with a look at contemporary debates in media and communications, arising particularly from developments in digital culture. Next the range of approaches to the increasingly used concept of mediation are explored, before I introduce and elaborate the three dimensions of mediation process which form the conceptual approach to the analysis of self-representation in digital culture taken in the book. The final part of the chapter shows how research on audiences is a key point of origin for the development of mediation as a concept with which to analyse self-representation.

Chapters 4–6 explore different sites of mediated self-representation, establishing both the ubiquity of self-representation and the variety of mediation processes shaping texts that are apparently alike. In Chapter 4 the role of broadcasters in producing self-representation in digital culture is explored. The first part of the chapter explores some of the challenges faced, and approaches taken, by broadcasting institutions in this time of digital culture. I then explore the BBC's forays into self-representation via BBC Wales' New Media Department's award-winning digital storytelling project, *Capture Wales*, looking in particular at how processes of textual mediation shape self-representations in this exemplary project. This is contrasted with moments of to-camera self-representation in other broadcast spaces, such as in the Channel Four reality TV programme *Faking It*, in which audience members learn (or fail to learn) to transform themselves.[7]

I discuss the ways in which the institutions of broadcasting in the era of digital culture are involved in facilitating, inviting, calling for and even demanding self-representation by ordinary members of their audience. I show how analyses of processes of textual, cultural and institutional mediation begin to reveal the social, cultural and political meanings of different self-representations across broadcast platforms. Considering the meaning of self-representations that might, at first glance, all look alike leads to questions of their political value – and here I mean to invoke both of the senses of the term 'political' discussed above (Mouffe, 2005).

In Chapter 5 the exploration of ubiquitous self-representation continues as I turn to consider museum and art worlds. In this chapter we see how at the very same time as museums face a crisis over their purpose and legitimacy, it has become commonplace for museum visitors to represent themselves in museum and arts spaces and in partnership with artists and art institutions. Here I explore a range of examples including funding bodies, artists and arts institutions. In particular I examine the Smithsonian in Washington DC, the Museum of London, and Bristol's Knowle West Media Centre/Arnolfini partnership with the American artist Suzanne Lacy. These examples show how it is that the analysis processes of institutional, cultural and textual mediation can uncover struggles in the meaning-making of self-representations of 'ordinary people'. The uncovering of these struggles serves to highlight, again, tensions over the worth of different kinds of self-representations and, consequently, as I suggest in the conclusion to this chapter, the thorny problem of the ascription of value.

In the last of the empirical discussions, I turn, in Chapter 6, to consider the promise of self-representation online. It is as if digital culture has allowed us to come as close as possible to the ideal of unmediated self-representation. At the beginning of this chapter I suggest that the internet is frequently seen as a site for less-mediated self-representation – of a kind requiring neither invitation, nor editing, nor publishing by media and cultural elites – and in this chapter I present a critique of this claim. I argue that self-representation is actually a condition of participation in Web 2.0. Moreover I suggest that rather than being less mediated, self-representation in Web 2.0 is subject to the same three dimensions of mediation process that shape self-representation everywhere that it is encountered – institutional, textual and cultural processes of mediation. The social networking site Facebook and the video-sharing site YouTube are taken as examples through which to unpack this argument. The concluding part of the chapter suggests that in a time of ubiquitous (and unavoidable) self-representation there is an urgent call for spaces explicitly addressing the problems of representation and media literacy – like the project of digital storytelling does.

The concluding Chapter 7 ('Self-Representation, Digital Culture and Genre') provides a response to the phenomena of ubiquitous self-representation discussed in the previous chapters. Here I recap on digital culture, the three dimensions of mediation and self-representation, before elaborating the idea of a genre of self-representation which, I suggest, emerges through the analysis in preceding chapters as a useful approach for uncovering the political, cultural and social meanings of the ubiquitous, apparently alike, but fundamentally different, self-representations with which we must increasingly contend – as scholars and as media audiences, cultural consumers and members of the public.

2
Histories of Self-Representation

Introduction

Representations tell stories and who tells what stories is a question of power. This chapter is concerned with the period from the nineteenth century to the contemporary, that is to say the early twenty-first century, a period during which representing ordinary people becomes a problem. The framework of the nation provides a useful lens through which to explore the changes in self-representation by 'ordinary people' over this period. This framework highlights the role of people as the public of a nation and the role of the very same people in undermining the coherence of the nation specifically because of the struggles with their limitations in their own representation.

In this chapter I offer an account of how social, cultural, political, economic and technological contexts have combined to bring about a proliferation of self-representation by members of the public in the contemporary moment. I argue against seeing this history as one of linear progress from the authority of the expert male voice to the authority of a plurality of ordinary people's voices; rather, the history is one of tension over the place and the use of other voices in the spaces of the cultural sphere. In the nineteenth century, national institutions assumed a clear authority about whose story counted and should be told. The history of the period from the nineteenth century to the present day can be understood as a history of successive assaults on that authority. It is a truism of contemporary historiography that the point of view of white upper- and middle-class men was challenged from within the nation by women, the working class and non-white populations, and from outside the nation by the populations in the rest of the world. Those attacks on the authority to narrate the nation can be seen in the ways in which the public was conceived and represented in the two major public service institutions in the cultural sphere – the museum and public service broadcasting – institutions that have been intimately involved in the construction and maintenance of the idea of national community (Bennett, 1995; Boswell and Evans, 1999; Corner and Harvey, 1991).

Central to attacks on the authority to narrate the nation was the disputation of the idea that the personal and experiential had no place in public discourse. In scholarly work, for example, theorists from a range of perspectives such as feminist theory, critical theory and media theory have reconsidered the place of experience in public discourse (see, for example, Code, 1993; Illouz, 2007; Mouffe, 1999; Van Zoonen, 2001). At the same time, commentators have noted the prevalence of the 'ordinary' voice of experience, so that, for example, the media scholar Jon Dovey refers to the 'self-speaking society' and the sociologist Ken Plummer to the society of the auto/biographical (Dovey, 2000; Plummer, 2001). In order to make sense of contemporary proliferating self-representations, then, we need first to look back.

I begin the historical account by turning to the birth of national cultural institutions as one of the key sites for the making of (national) publics. It is clear that the making of the national public involved tensions surrounding the cultural representation of that public. How is a public to be represented and how does 'the public' refer to or exclude the ordinary person? In this chapter I trace some of the ways in which the tensions surrounding ordinary people's representation were responded to – responses that worked within, outside and against national institutional structures. The case of the UK is explored in some detail as a useful exemplar of the issues that have arisen in this history of representing ordinary people. Of course, this is by no means to argue that the UK case can be neatly extrapolated to the histories of other countries, but we can nevertheless see how certain issues (that are clearly not limited to the UK) arise and are addressed in the cultural history of that nation.

In what follows, I explore representations of 'the people' from the nineteenth century through to a time when people are 'representing themselves' across a phenomenal range of settings in contemporary life. Today, self-representations appear both within and beyond the frameworks of national institutions and their publics. Before exploring the history of ordinary people's cultural representation, I address the slippery but central concepts of 'ordinary people' and 'community'.

Constructing ordinary people and community

Ordinary people

Raymond Williams' *Keywords* provides a starting point for considering the use of the term 'ordinary people' (Williams, 1983). Building on Williams' discussion, we can identify four broad senses of the term: denigration; celebration; everyday; citizenry. These are absolutely not neat categories but are nevertheless important to identify because they invoke quite different meanings in the notion of the ordinary person.

Firstly, 'ordinary' is used in a denigratory sense in which people are defined as ordinary because of their inferior position in a hierarchy. Here 'ordinary' is equated with ignorance and defined in opposition to 'expert', which is equated with possession of knowledge. Or, 'ordinary people' might be evoked in opposition to unusual people, special people and extraordinary people. In this sense 'ordinary' can also imply banal, dull and mundane. 'Ordinary people' have long been invoked in a denigratory sense in the notion of the 'mass' and here the term often functions as a euphemism for working class (Adorno and Horkheimer, 1993 (1944)). The notion of the mass implies an undifferentiated group and 'ordinary people', used in this sense, denies distinctiveness and difference. Couldry's suggestion of a 'pervasive' division between 'media worlds' and 'ordinary worlds' (Couldry, 2000a) suggests that the term 'ordinary people' operates not only to denigrate, but also to categorise and contain.

Secondly, 'ordinary' is *claimed* in a *celebratory* sense in direct reaction against the negative portrayal discussed above. In this sense 'ordinary people' are valued precisely *because* they have been marginalised. Here again, 'ordinary person' can also operate as a euphemism for working class, as in the phrase 'voices from below' found in the rhetoric surrounding the collection of oral history, for example. The celebratory sense of the term 'ordinary people' indicates a political position – one which disputes whose account of reality matters. The oral history movement can be understood, in this light, as being motivated by the argument that the history of the general public is as important as the official history of rulers, politicians and the like. But 'ordinary people' is used in this celebratory sense to invoke any number of marginalised groups, indicating a tension between the notion of 'ordinary' and the notion of difference. Can everyone be 'ordinary' while also being different? For example, on the one hand, the British National Party invokes the notion of 'ordinary people' to *unite* white, working-class British people and to *exclude* others; on the other hand, public service projects that invite members of the public to represent themselves invoke 'ordinary people' to argue that everyone's life is central to the historical record of a society. Here, 'ordinary people' is used to unite across difference. The term is used in the celebratory sense, then, to unite groups of people based on shared marginality from positions of social and political power in societies.

Thirdly, the everyday sense of 'ordinary people' describes the use of the term to refer to *people* whose *practices* are 'ordinary'. In this sense 'ordinary people' again operates as a *claim*. But in this usage the claim is to declare that people who might seem different, in fact have much in common, they too are all 'ordinary'. The sense of 'ordinary people' as those who live everyday life claims commonality, even equality, and denies difference between people. Yet, Ben Highmore's (2002) observation that the everyday is also the home of the bizarre and the mysterious highlights a paradox in this everyday sense of 'ordinary people'. Moreover, as Highmore notes, the idea of the everyday is itself problematic, since we need to ask – everyday for whom? While Harvey Sacks suggested that we continually reaffirm our 'ordinariness' by speaking from recognisably personal perspectives in an understandably 'ordinary' way (Sacks, 1984, p. 429), Michael Billig argued that conversation analysis fails to address inequalities in conversation and society which problematise the unifying project of 'ordinary' (Billig, 1999, p. 554). Emmanuel Schegloff, responding to Billig, regards difference and distinction as factors emerging from time to time, but not rendering the notion of 'ordinary' (as everyday) inherently problematic (Schegloff, 1999, p. 566).

Lastly, we can discern a use of the term ordinary people which locates ordinary people as the citizens of democracy – the citizenry, the public. Here, 'ordinary people' functions to invoke people as a political force, as in the phrase 'the people'. John Durham Peters notes that, in the bourgeois public sphere, 'the personal characteristics of the speaker must be irrelevant to participation and critique' (1993, p. 551). When 'ordinary people' are invoked to mean 'the citizenry', the term is used in opposition to the notion of 'the masses'. The use of the term 'ordinary person' to mean 'citizen' is used to argue that public service institutions should *represent* citizens, as well as informing and educating them (see above). This sense of 'ordinary people' also figures in the subsequent debate about how well the public is being represented, that is, in evaluating how exactly members of the public are represented. Are such representations, for example, biased and stereotypical, or fair and truthful?

On the one hand the term 'ordinary people' is used to unite given groups of people under the unifying heading 'ordinary', so that, for example, working-class people might be pulled together under the heading 'ordinary people' across racial and ethnic divides and, in this way, 'ordinary' works to smooth out or ignore problems caused by difference. On the other hand, 'ordinary people' unites people as a group in distinction to those who are not 'ordinary' and thus the term actually marks difference. In any case most usage of the term 'ordinary people' slips between these meanings and uses the slippage in some way, hence the rhetorical and symbolic power of the construction 'ordinary person' to support arguments and make claims.

Academic debate about the presence of 'ordinary people' in cultural representations has revolved around whether we are witnessing a kind of poor imitation of what 'real' representation might look like. The debate concerns *why* the representation is there, its veracity and authenticity, and the extent to which it can be seen as a proper representation versus the extent to which it might be seen as publicity – in Habermasean terms, a managed show, populism, pandering, for example, to the discourse of community and participation which currently appears dominant (Habermas, 1974, 1989). Debate about access, literacy and citizenship all invoke 'ordinary people' as the *citizenry*. While questions about how members of the public are represented in a democracy have acquired new dimensions in the context of digital culture, they are nonetheless longstanding ones in debates about the role of public cultural institutions like museums and public service broadcasting, particularly factual broadcasting. The figure of the 'ordinary person' has long loomed large in these debates, as we shall see.

Community

I have argued that the members of the public who appear in contemporary media are constructed as ordinary people. The next part of my argument is to suggest that a second construct often shapes these representations: that of the *community*, since the participating public are frequently understood as located in (various kinds of) 'communities'. The term 'community' has common sense meaning and is used as a descriptive term, as in the now ubiquitous phrase 'working with communities'. It is assumed to be self-evident that we all know what this means. In common with the construct 'ordinary people', the construct 'community' always operates as a claim (Silverstone, 1999). 'Community', like 'ordinary person', is both an emotive and a slippery concept.

'Community', as Williams has noted, conjures an image of people rather than institutions (1983). For Benedict Anderson, 'community' is the work of a collective imagination which is tightly articulated with imagining the nation. He writes 'the nation is always conceived as a deep, horizontal comradeship' (Anderson, 1991, p. 7). For Anderson, then, 'community' refers to a kind of *comradeship* that rests on a shared (*imagined*) history (and future). Anderson describes how the press functioned to sustain a symbolic *national* community. But to say it was symbolic is not to suggest that it was not also lived, as Silverstone notes,

> Communities are lived. But also imagined. And if people believe something to be real, then as the American sociologist W.I. Thomas famously noted, it is real in its consequences. Ideas of community hover between experience and desire.
>
> (1999, p. 97)

Anderson highlighted the role of the press in sustaining the idea of a national community and, as Roger Silverstone notes, the rise of other mass media, notably the radio, further fulfilled this function

(Silverstone, 1999, p. 100). The idea of national community is central to the very idea of public service institutions in the cultural sphere and representing members of the public becomes important to what public service institutions in the cultural domain are understood as being *for*, as discussed in Chapter 3.

As many scholars have pointed out, the notion of community was always problematic because it is necessarily exclusionary (e.g. Bauman, 2001; Hall, 1999). As a result, 'national community' is a notion that must be continually reconstructed, through, for example, institutions like public museums and public service broadcasting. Jeffrey C. Alexander and Ronald N. Jacobs have noted that communications media are vitally important for the construction and maintenance of connection across peoples in differentiated societies. They argue that what they describe as the 'realm of symbolic communication' is a vital function of the public sphere in civil society. For Alexander and Jacobs, where the size of our societies means that actual interaction with everyone is impossible, the maintenance of the 'symbolic realm' depends on the media and, in particular, on the media's ritualistic function (Alexander and Jacobs, 1998).

Perhaps the national community cannot exist, or be represented, in the contemporary fragmented and diversified media environment, as Silverstone notes,

> As a result of these developments, the minority and the local, the critical and the global, it is possible to suggest that the first and most significant casualty will be national community.
>
> (1999, p. 103)

The problems that the idea of national community glossed over, as, for example, the problem of racism (Hall, 1999), may now have fractured the idea of national community. This suggests that Todd Gitlin's concept of 'public sphericules' has more explanatory power in the contemporary moment than does the notion of the national community (Gitlin, 1998). However, while it has been observed that the affordances of digital culture further enable the proliferation of 'public sphericules', the consequences for groupings across nations, and also internationally, are not cut and dried. Thus, as Bart Cammaerts notes, drawing on Held and McGrew (2002), and Tarrow (2005), separate groups can and do come together to cooperate:

> As the World Social Forum and many coordinated actions against international organizations show, fragmentation does not per se exclude strategic cooperation between very different civil society associations – from very loose activist networks to structured and professional civil society organizations, labor unions, or even political parties, from revolutionary movements to reformist movements (Held and McGrew, 2002; Tarrow, 2005).
>
> (Cammaerts, 2007, p. 265)

In the context of proliferating communities, which separate and unite at different moments and for different and complex reasons, national public service institutions continue to invite members of the public to represent themselves, constructing them as ordinary people and locating them in seemingly fixed 'communities'. The question, then, is – how is the construct *'communities'* functioning in these kinds of project and why is this a key term at a time when it has become so troubled? In discussing what she calls 'community's resuscitation in recent debates' (Mayo, 2006, p. 388), Marjorie Mayo refers to Sennett's earlier argument:

> 'The Fall of Public Man' (Sennett, 1976) started from the erosion of public life, the self-absorption and the alienation accompanying late twentieth century capitalism. In response, community became a 'problem on people's minds', Sennett pointed out (Sennett, 1976: 298).
>
> (Mayo, 2006, p. 389)

Silverstone, Bauman and Mayo, among others, have pointed to the current ubiquity of the term 'community' and have linked this ubiquity to the individualised, fragmented and insecure nature of life in contemporary societies. Mayo, drawing on Anthony Giddens (1991), emphasises that the argument is not to suggest that life was once more secure, or community more real, but rather that 'individuals are expected to take responsibility for themselves and their families' (Mayo, 2006, p. 390). Mayo goes on to link the current situation to the neo-liberal political and economic policies that dominate the globe, and the so-called Post-Washington Consensus. The Post-Washington Consensus, in economic and development circles, and particularly in the World Bank, is the name given to the consensus (from the mid-1990s) that social programmes tackling poverty and exclusion should be used to temper the free rein of the market. Suzanne Bergeron notes that the ideas favoured under the heading 'Post-Washington Consensus' meant including consideration of cultural and social context, but she emphasises that this was consideration of cultural context in order to make economic policies more effective (Bergeron, 2003). The 'Post-Washington Consensus' followed the earlier 'Washington Consensus', which was the title given to the argument in favour of parties across the political spectrum, and across the globe, agreeing on the promotion of neo-liberal economic policy, described by the originator of the term as 'good economics' (Williamson, 1993, p. 1330). In describing what has become known as the Post-Washington Consensus, Mayo writes,

> And by the mid to late nineties there were increasing expressions of concern about the need to mitigate the negative effects of too rampant neo-liberalism, concerns that were expressed internationally (via United Nations Human Development Reports for example) as well as by national governments and by voluntary and community organisations and agencies.
>
> (2006, p. 392)

Mayo suggests that it is in this context that we have seen what she describes as 'community as policy'. I suggest that it is in the same context that the two constructs 'ordinary people' and 'community' have played a central role in shaping the self-representations of members of the public in those projects that are run by publicly funded institutions. It remains a question as to whether, and how, the concepts 'ordinary people' and 'community' shape other kinds of self-representations across contemporary digital culture such as, for example, those that appear as part of reality TV, advertising, social networking or video-sharing websites; that is, are the people who are representing themselves in these other sites still constructed as ordinary people and located (or fixed) in communities? Is 'ordinary people in community' a feature of publicly funded self-representation or a feature of *all* self-representation? I return to this question in concluding Chapter 7. The remainder of the present chapter addresses the history of representations of ordinary people both within and beyond the boundaries of national communities.

Constructing the public, building the nation

The end of the eighteenth century is widely regarded as the moment of the creation and construction of the idea of the nation in the west (see, for example, Anderson, 1991). Nation-building took place in earnest in the western democracies in the nineteenth century. As Anderson demonstrates, the nation was as much a construction in imaginary and symbolic terms as in any concrete sense. It was vital that the idea of the nation was adopted by the population of the nation – the public. Representing the nation to the public was the key to fostering and encouraging national belonging and the very idea of nation.

Scholars suggest that the museum institution was central to the making of the nation in the nineteenth century. Thus Martin Prosler notes: 'The museum was one of those spaces within which the nation could present itself as an "imagined community" (Anderson, 1991 [1983]) in all possible aspects' (Prosler, 1996, p. 32). This national community must by definition be a community with borders, so that, crucially, the western nation was imagined against that which it was not:

> In parallel to this the creation of ethnological museums based on the cultures of 'uncivilised peoples', and the introduction of colonial pavilions at world exhibitions, served to chart a difference between peoples and hence reinforce a national consciousness during the phase of the definition of a 'standard of civilisation'.
>
> (1996, p. 34)

Thus the purpose of museums was to represent people *within* the nation, while at the same time museums represented people *outside* the nation; the museum served to clarify national boundaries. In this way museums helped to define the nation by representing who was understood to belong and who was not.

The British Museum opened (to a limited extent) to the public in 1759 (McLean, 1997; Schubert, 2000). Provision of public museums grew throughout the nineteenth and early twentieth centuries (see, for example, Bennett, 1995; Prosler, 1996; Walsh, 1992). However, as Andrea Witcomb observes about this period, '[t]he museum is mostly seen as inculcating bourgeois civic values that served the needs of the emerging nation-state and the dominant interests within it' (Witcomb, 2003, p. 14). Indeed, Fiona McLean notes of the earliest (so-called) public museums,

> The predilection for housing museums in grand buildings, reminiscent of a gentleman's private residence, did nothing to encourage public participation. Nor did the curtailing of access in many of the early museums. Museums were not universally regarded as catering 'for the public benefit' (Museums Association 1984) – there was no immediate right of entry.
>
> (1997, p. 11)

The world fairs of the nineteenth century, beginning with the Great Exhibition in London in 1851, changed perceptions about the museum audience:

> These exhibitions attracted vast numbers of people, who were able to visit them with the advent of the railway age. These trade fairs persuaded governments that museums could be used as a means of social utility and social control; the population could use their spare time constructively by visiting museums and educating themselves, becoming more civilized in the process.
>
> (1997, p. 12)

Similarly, Tony Bennett notes a change in the purpose of museums in the mid-nineteenth century:

> The mid-nineteenth century reconceptualization of museums as public resources that might be deployed as governmental instruments involving the whole population thus entailed a significant revaluation of earlier cultural strategies. In the earlier phase, the rules and proscriptions governing attendance at museums had served to distinguish the bourgeois public from the rough and

raucous manners of the general populace by excluding the latter. By contrast, the museum's new conception as an instrument of public instruction envisaged it as, in its new openness, an exemplary space in which the rough and raucous might learn to civilize themselves by modelling their conduct on the middle-class codes of behavior to which museum attendance would expose them.

(Bennett, 1995, p. 28)

Bennett draws on Foucault's ideas about governmentality to argue that the purpose of museums was one where 'culture is brought within the province of government, its conception is on a par with other regions of government' (1995, p. 18). He draws on Habermas' historical work, noting museums role (as part of art and culture) in the formation of the bourgeois public sphere. He writes that it was this public sphere 'in whose name the subsequent development of the debased public sphere of mass culture could be castigated', arguing that 'the public' was partly *constituted by* the museum (1995). Bennett suggests that the role of museums in the formation of the bourgeois public sphere laid the way for museums to be used in the service of governance. We shall return to ideas about *governance* and *publics* in concluding the study of mediated self-representation in Chapter 7.

Early museums represented 'uncivilised peoples' as a way to define the civilised population of the nation. But crucially the 'civilised' population of the nation did not include everyone living in the nation; museums were sites where it was hoped the working classes would learn to emulate the 'civilised' middle classes. While fairgrounds were associated with the working classes and popular 'mass' culture, museums were associated with the middle classes, high culture and education. Although there is debate as to the extent to which the working classes attended museums, it is clear that nineteenth-century museums were places that educated the national population *about* the nation and how to be a 'proper' member of the nation. The point of view of members of the public of different class and gender, or indeed racial and ethnic, backgrounds was not understood as part of the national story; rather, a unifying (and therefore silencing) story of the nation was told from the perspective of white middle-class male authority – as suggested at the start of this chapter; many (or even most) inhabitants of the newly constructed nation did not see themselves reflected in these institutions. And certainly, populations of the colonies of the empire did not see themselves represented as belonging within those walls.

Debating the public, broadening the nation

Public service broadcasting in the early twentieth century was seen as a vehicle for promotion of the so-called public interest; this effectively meant the construction and sustenance of national, mass audiences who would constitute 'the public'. In this way, through its address, public service broadcasting joined museums in the continuing project of constructing the nation state. In the 1920s USA, as Marc Raboy notes, a kind of public service broadcasting was secured with the Federal Radio Act of 1927 (Raboy, 2008). In the UK after the General Strike of 1926, one of the earliest of the many BBC reviews, by the Crawford Committee, recommended (as had the first review, by the Sykes Committee of 1923) that the BBC be nationalised (BBC *Committees of Enquiry*, n.d.; Born, 2004; Smith, 1974). Thus, public service broadcasting in Britain began with the formation of the BBC 'as a state-regulated monopoly in 1927' (Scannell, 1996a).

In the UK, the BBC spoke to the nation, first via radio and subsequently also via TV, as John Ellis writes,

> Through the idea of public service broadcasting, broadcasting became another tool in the construction of the nation state. As such, it joined earlier forces of social unification: the construction of railways, the standardization of clock time, the drive towards universal literacy, the standardization of working practices and holiday entitlements, the development of universal suffrage, the development of a national press.
>
> (2000, p. 51)

In the early years the broadcaster claimed to address an inclusive national population. Thus Anthony Smith, describing the origins of broadcasting with the invention of wireless telephony in the 1890s, argued that the BBC addressed a national public which included all social classes:

There had been a relaxation of the barriers between classes and a widespread realisation existed that information, as well as entertainment, no longer needed to be circulated within proscribed class lines. There was, therefore, the beginning of a conception of the national audience as a mass audience. The new journalism and the new entertainment encouraged and nurtured this incipient feeling.

(Smith, 1974, p. 20)

Because it claimed to speak to (and consequently constructed) the national public, early broadcasting always faced questions about who constituted the public and what the appropriate way to fulfil a public service mandate might be. Thus with the inception of public service broadcasting, seeds for the activity of *self-representation* were sown in anxieties about institutional purposes and specifically the question of *how* to *represent* the public. Smith's edited compilation of reports by and about the BBC illustrates this point:

As broadcasting developed into a double medium, and television joined radio to create extremely powerful concentrations of cultural power in each society, the problems of how to organise the medium, how to finance it, how to supervise it and *how to allow the public some kind of representation within it* multiplied the perplexities which had been present from the beginning.

(1974, p. 14) (my italics)

Furthermore decentralisation was recommended as early as 1935 by the Ullswater Committee (BBC *Committees of Enquiry*, n.d., p. 2) and reiterated in later reviews, and the Beveridge Committee of 1949 raised the question of the representation of minority views (p. 3).

The question of how exactly to represent the public in cultural institutions was an abiding area of contestation. Moreover, this struggle can be seen being played out in the earlier practices of institutions, which, today, converge on the facilitation of self-representation by the public. Museums, booming in the nineteenth century, carefully prescribed a kind of public that excluded many of the population, emphasising middle-class values as the ones to be adopted by anybody entering the space. Moreover, as we have seen, museums were a part of transnational projects of national construction with global ramifications (Karp et al., 2006). While early museum professionals may not have been concerned with the question of whom they excluded, they nevertheless created exclusions, giving rise to counter-narratives and counter-representations. And notions of high and low culture (and the associated class-based audiences) worried proponents of public service broadcasting in ways that echo anxieties about mass culture and the educational, reforming (and controlling) role of the museum. While, as we have seen, nineteenth-century museums claimed to address the national public, but hoped to 'civilise' those members of the working class who did venture into their spaces, early public service broadcasting was discussed in terms of an educational role and was critiqued when it was seen as pandering to 'the lowest common denominator'. As Frances Bonner writes of the Reithian remit to 'inform, educate, and entertain',

> In some of the earlier enunciations of this mission, especially when in a political context, such as over the introduction of television, it was apparent that 'entertain' was very much the least of the three, only really a sweetener for the real activities of education and information.
>
> (2003, p. 22)

Moreover, debate about the *meaning* of *culture*, and, specifically, critique of the dominant Reithian definition of culture, was also always a part of public service broadcasting as it developed in the UK, and indeed as it developed in other nation states around the globe, many of whom followed the UK model to various extents. Today's anxieties about cultural production, mass culture and representation are unsurprisingly not new. Captain Peter Eckersley, the chief engineer of the early BBC, noted in his memoirs,

> The BBC of those days is to be congratulated because it took a line which its directors considered was in the best interests of the public and not necessarily commercially beneficial to the wireless trade. The company undoubtedly saw itself as a great cultural

force, by which it meant something uniquely constituted to avoid the postures of vulgarity. The unfortunate thing, to my mind, was that its idea of becoming a cultural force was so uncultured. P.P Eckersley. The Power Behind the Microphone (1942), 48.

(1974, pp. 53–4)

Unlike museums, however, public service broadcasting has a history of actually representing 'ordinary people'. Paddy Scannell's, and Scannell and David Cardiff's work suggests that the notion of the 'ordinary person' played a key role in early British radio and TV. They argue that there were explicit and conscious representations of 'ordinary people' throughout the early years (Scannell, 1996b; Scannell and Cardiff, 1991). Here 'ordinary people' is invoked in the everyday sense: 'broadcasting produced and produces itself as part of and as for the everyday world, for that is the world in which listeners and viewers ordinarily live' (Scannell, 1996b, p. 89). Clearly we should not overstress the parallels between the institutions of the museum and those of broadcasting – early museums were most definitely not part of the everyday world, but rather constructed the ideal world, the imagined community of the nation – with its imagined history as well. The role of technology is obviously of key importance here – radio and TV occupied the everyday space of the living room inside people's homes while museums typically occupied grand residences signalling and celebrating the greatness of the nation in their architecture and in their interior design. We can start to see how necessary the analytic concept of mediation is to understanding self-representation, historically and contemporarily, in the myriad cultural settings in which it now appears.

While museums continued to construct the ideal national story through excluding differing perspectives, a perception of inadequate representation of the public within media spaces continued through the early years of broadcasting and was addressed in various ways. Indeed John Corner places the category of the 'ordinary person' at the heart of documentary practice from the Grierson-led movement of the 1930s onwards, suggesting that this cinema explicitly valorised the category of the ordinary:

a declared belief in modern citizenship, unprejudiced by older, class hierarchic values and newly committed to exploring 'ordinary life' as part of a proper representation of community and nation.

(Corner, 1995a, p. 82)

Similarly, Highmore describes the later 1930s *Mass Observation* project as an explicit response to the way that ordinary people were hitherto represented (2002). Highmore argues that rather than imposing class-based categories on participants, *Mass Observation* allowed nuanced versions of class affiliation to emerge (ibid.).

Representing the public, limitations of the nation

Debate continued over *how* to represent the public properly. Anxiety over representation of the public is central to Richard Hoggart's celebrated 1957 *Uses of Literacy* (Hoggart, 1957). Hoggart suggested that the construct 'ordinary person' is *used* to suit economic imperatives. He suggested (as did mid-Victorian critics before him, according to Mark Hampton's (2001) account) that representations of 'ordinary everyday life' are an exploitative replacement of the opportunity for meaningful, rational participation in society (Hampton, 2001; Hoggart, 1957). Williams' 1958 article, 'Culture is Ordinary', also places the construct of the 'ordinary person' at the centre of the debate about how cultural representation is shaped by economic imperatives. But Williams claimed value for the 'ordinary' in culture, where culture had more commonly hitherto been understood as 'high' culture (Williams, 2002 (1958)). Gareth Palmer takes further the classed dimension of this arguing that, from its inception in the 1950s, British TV documentary involved middle-class producers representing working-class people for consumption by middle-class audiences (2002). In this view, ordinary people are not only constructed and displayed for economic motives, but also ordinary people are a euphemism for working-class people and such representations are made for, and consumed by, middle-class people. In these arguments, we can observe the centrality of the contested and slippery construct 'ordinary' discussed earlier in this chapter.

From the 1960s, the oral history movement internationally, the Direct Cinema movement in the US and Cinéma Vérité in France all addressed a lack of adequate public representation. Corner suggests that the Direct Cinema movement in the US and Cinéma Vérité in

France offered a specific response to a perceived failure in existing representation of 'ordinary people' – both movements claiming to represent 'ordinary people' with *minimal mediation*. Corner suggests that these movements influenced subsequent documentary TV and the development of access TV in 1970s UK (1994). Corner describes Access:

> we can say that access is the avoiding or the correcting of imbalances in broadcasting's representation of politics and society by the articulation of a diversity of 'directly' stated views from different sections of the public and by the reflection, again 'directly', of the real diversity of cultural, social and economic circumstances, particularly those which require attention and action.
>
> (1994, p. 22)

Ordinary people are here conceived of in a celebratory sense because the purpose of Access is to celebrate or validate the reality of those lives, through enabling self-representation and, in so doing, arguing for social change (1994). The explicitly political view also invokes the citizenry sense of the term 'ordinary people'. These movements – oral history, Cinéma Vérité, Direct Cinema and the early forms of Access TV in the UK – were *all* explicitly political and *all* drew on both the citizenry and the celebratory senses of the term 'ordinary people'.

Access and the other examples discussed here take place firmly inside national institutional systems – national systems of public service broadcasting or particular national cinema systems. But we can also identify attempts to represent ordinary people which were not situated within national frameworks or indeed explicitly attempted to cut across such frameworks and to invoke different kinds of groupings. Pamela Wilson and Michelle Stewart note the impact of Direct Cinema and Cinéma Vérité movements on the representation of indigenous people, arguing that the failures of these, supposedly minimally mediated representations, convinced of the need for self-representation:

> Thus by setting up a camera and allowing the film to roll, some ethnographic filmmakers sought to document indigenous cultural practices objectively. The excesses and absurdity of the worst

of these practices led ethnographers and Indigenous groups to develop an ethos and practice of dialogic filmmaking and anthropological advocacy and convinced many of the necessity for self-representation.

(Wilson and Stewart, 2008, p. 4)

Direct Cinema and Cinéma Vérité, as movements which aimed to address the limits of previous filmic representations, led to more direct kinds of representation within *and against* nations.

It is important to emphasise the fact that these movements frequently used personal perspective and personal experience, and in so doing they politicised the personal *experience* of members of the public/ordinary people. Michael Renov, writing about the US context, observes a growth of self-representation in documentary film practice, linking it particularly to the influences of second-wave feminism:

the work of later practitioners bears the marks of a radical shift of values associated with the emergence of second-wave feminism by the early 1970s. A new foregrounding of the politics of everyday life encouraged the interrogation of identity and subjectivity and of a vividly corporeal rather than intellectualised self.

(2004, p. 171)

And the subject produced in these representations was one which *did not* put national affiliation and national identity at its core identification.

At the same time, in the museums field, there had been the establishment of museums that 'spoke back' to the nations in which they were situated, arguing for a space for representation, spaces which became cause for arguments and campaigns over who they should rightly represent as surrounding populations change. Thus Kratz and Karp note that there are many such examples globally and discuss these in their edited collection *Museum Frictions Public Cultures/Global Transformation*. They write,

Some ethnic and community-based museums in the United States, for example, are torn between competing tasks: developing programs for audiences with forms of self-consciousness derived

from transnational migrations and diasporas, yet also following
missions defined and associated with their history as museums
fundamentally grounded in local and national concerns.

(Kratz and Karp, 2006, p. 7)

This collection of essays on global museums encompasses scholarship on the widest imaginable range of museums, from voluntary-
run, privately funded to state-funded, to endowment-funded, to
public–private partnership, and in many places around the world.
The collection makes absolutely clear that we cannot possibly gen-
eralise about how museums across the globe are dealing with the
challenges of contemporary politics, economics, technology, culture
and society in their various settings. Nevertheless there do appear to
be some shared problems (and indeed possibilities), some of which
speak directly to the concerns of this book. Most interesting is the
crisis (that has been growing over time) over the idea of a coherent,
singular story of a nation, which was fundamental to the formation of the national museum. This is by no means to argue that
the nation has disappeared or become irrelevant. On the contrary, it
is the continued power and importance of the national idea, combined with the reality of diverse (and transnational) populations
that exceed this idea, which seems to be the challenge facing cultural institutions of museums and indeed public broadcasting or, as
many are suggesting we now call it, public communications (see, for
example, Raboy, 2008).

Publics represent themselves inside, outside and against the nation

Ellis suggested at the turn of the twenty-first century that the history of TV can be roughly divided into three eras: 'scarcity' (up to
the late 1970s or early 1980s); 'availability' (from the early 1980s);
'plenty' (the future of TV or 'content' as predicted by the industry)
(Ellis, 2000). Of the era of scarcity, Ellis notes,

This was another aspect of television's era of scarcity: a small
group of adepts, the programme-makers, were accumulating practical knowledge of the effects of the process of witness, but these

knowledges had no wider currency. In the age of scarcity, television came from an elite, and it remained an honour for anyone outside that elite to be invited to appear on the screen.

(Ellis, 2000, p. 51)

Cultural institutions of museums and broadcasting have responded to changing political and economic policies, technological developments and, perhaps most of all, to characteristics associated with the period of late-modernity or post-modernity by moving towards displaying a multiplicity of representations, including self-representations. Moreover, these institutional productions join, as we began to discuss in the last section, a phenomenal proliferation of self-representations across a dizzying array of kinds of space globally, whose points of reference move beyond, and against, the nation and which are always mediated by institutional, textual and cultural processes, producing, as we shall see in the following chapters, problematic, promising and even pretend, representations of selves – by ordinary people.

Accounts of both public sector museums and broadcasting situate changes in their roles over time in the context of a post-modern failure of grand narratives and coterminous rise of multiculturalism, or in the context of a more gradual transition from enlightenment to modernity and late-modernity. However labelled, this historical period is undoubtedly associated with growing individualisation (Beck, 1992; Giddens, 1991). And, as Plummer has described in the phrase 'auto/biographical society', this individualisation is associated with a growth in the telling of *stories* of individuals (Plummer, 2001).

The move towards self-representation takes place in a historical trajectory that emphasises a profound anxiety surrounding the role of national cultural institutions in the late-twentieth century (see, for example, museum debates; Hudson, 1999; Karp et al., 2006; Macdonald, 1996; Urry, 1996; Walsh, 1992). In the mid-nineties Macdonald summed up the anxieties facing museology:

Most of museums' long-held assumptions and functions have been challenged over the last decade or so; and at the same time the boundaries between museums and other institutions have become elided such that museum professionals can declare: 'The

truth is, we do not know any more what a museum institution is'
(Sola, 1992: 106).

(Macdonald, 1996, p. 1)

Processes described at the end of the twentieth century have only
intensified into the twenty-first century. One of the ways in which
contemporary museum and cultural institutions (from the national
to the local) resolve this anxiety is by inviting members of the public
to *speak for themselves.* In so doing, contemporary museums construct the public as a self-representing public. And at the same time
they render the question of how self-representations are mediated a
critical one.

In a *Consultation on Museums in the 21st Century* in 2005, Tessa
Jowell, then UK Secretary of State for Culture, Media and Sport
(DCMS), called for the role of museums in the governance of the
public to be enhanced and strengthened:

> But for me, and the Government, they [museums] are something
> much more: a way for us to see our place in the world. This is
> all the more important as society changes, and new values of
> nationality and community emerge. The fixed points of history
> and heritage have an even greater meaning as our world becomes
> smaller, and our values develop.
>
> (DCMS, 2005, p. 3)

Here is a call for a traditional governmental role for museums. But
this call is tempered by the suggestion that we are in a time where
'new values of nationality and community emerge'. Jowell's remarks
capture contemporary uncertainty regarding authoritative accounts
of history, and indeed of nation, at a time when museology favours
the expression of a multiplicity of viewpoints. Funding bodies currently deploy a similar discourse of engaging the public in telling
their own stories as part of the 'new values of nationality and
community':

> Arts Council England's ambition for 2006–8 is to put the arts
> at the heart of national life and people at the heart of the
> arts. [...] We will ensure that more high quality work reaches

a wider range of people – engaging them as both audience and participants.

(Arts Council, 2008)

When one explores the kinds of project which have been taking place, it is clear that the *participation* referred to frequently takes the form of *self-representation*, taking up Walsh's earlier suggestion that

A new museology must concern itself with involving the public, not just during the visit to the museum through interactive displays, but also in the production of their own pasts.

(1992, p. 161)

This assertion demonstrates that a discourse of (cultural) citizenship and self-representation was already emerging in the early 1990s, emphasising a historical account drawing on personal, familial *experience* (1992, p. 167).

Much later, Message and Healy similarly suggest that a 'central focus on emotion is one of the ways in which the NMA [National Museum of Australia] marks itself as a new museum' (2004, p. 1). Emotional and experiential accounts are offered as trustworthy precisely *because* they do not claim to be objective. Further, such accounts are synonymous with the representation of 'ordinary', 'everyday life'. This has clear implications for the kind of public constructed: while the idea of self-representation invokes a democratic discourse of individual rights, the therapeutic discourse signalled by the privileging of experience is what self-representation often seems to imply in practice. Thus, taking up his own earlier concept of 'exhibitionary complex', Bennett has suggested that contemporary museums are characterised by the museum institution's formation in modernity, its particular version of what Bennett calls 'the logic of culture' and, most importantly for my argument, its use of participation, or as Bennett puts it,

a commitment to dialogic and multisensory forms of visitor engagement that have challenged the authoritarian and ocular-centric forms of didacticism that characterized the earlier organization of the exhibitory complex.

(2006, p. 57)

The question of whether the valorisation of experience facilitates a democratic function has already been addressed in the context of TV. Murdock argued in 1999 that participation rights, which have led to self-representation by publics and a focus on experience, have not led to meaningful participation in TV but, instead, have seen the 'aggressive promotion of ordinariness which fits snugly with the political economy of the new commercialism' (1999, p. 15). Scholars responding to the deregulation in broadcasting during the late 1980s and early 1990s have used the representation of the 'ordinary person' in their critique of the quality of representation. Murdock shares the view of many when he puts together the proliferation of material featuring 'ordinary people' with the need to make inexpensive programmes to fill the hours (1999). In this way, a perceived proliferation of the 'ordinary' is seen as an example of the populism and exploitation which, it is claimed, characterise contemporary media (ibid.). There is widespread anxiety that experiential forms of factual programming have replaced informative and critical ones, and in this discussion there is a tendency to accept a binary opposition between knowledge and experience. The terms 'ordinary' and 'quality' are often used as shorthand to describe the commercialisation of programming and this is 'ordinary' in a denigratory sense (see, for example, Corner et al., 1994). Thus Murdock writes,

> They have replaced paternalism's hierarchies of capacity and insight with the open horizons of populism, which celebrates common sense as the only sense worth having and presents audience size as the only valid criterion of communicative success.
>
> (1999, p. 15)

The 'ordinary person' is particularly central to discussions of reality TV, a kind of programming which continues to dominate public service and commercial channels alike globally (e.g. Hill, 2005; Hill et al., 2002, 2007; Van Zoonen, 2001). Couldry has suggested that reality TV programmes function to reconstruct the hierarchical distinction between 'ordinary' and 'media' worlds (Couldry, 2002). On the other hand, Van Zoonen argued that *Big Brother*'s representation of 'ordinary people' indicates an exciting shift in terms of which issues are deemed to be of public concern: 'Each of those formats has been subjected to similar criticism: one should not flaunt private emotions, nor does one relish observing these emotions' (Van Zoonen, 2001, p. 672). Van Zoonen argues that this critique is based on the separation of public and private, suggesting that the popularity of reality TV indicates that such separation is no longer either acceptable or functional (ibid.). Although Van Zoonen deploys the term 'ordinary' in the everyday sense to refer to 'ordinary daily humdrum experience' (2001, p. 673), she also uses 'ordinary' in the celebratory sense, whereby 'ordinary' is equated with the private sphere and hence with experience that had been excluded from view because of the bourgeois division between public and private. And, for Van Zoonen, reality TV's representation of 'ordinary people' constitutes an exciting development for democracy; this, then, is 'ordinary people' in the citizenry sense.

In their seminal study of talk show participation, *Talk on Television*, Livingstone and Lunt suggested that ordinary people are given a platform from which to make public their usually marginal/hidden experience and here ordinary people are invoked in the celebratory sense. But, in Livingstone and Lunt's account, ordinary people are constituted as 'ordinary' at least in part because of the personal, psychological and individual perspectives from which they speak – implying that there are limits to the kinds of 'ordinariness' that can be represented (1994). Political positions, group formation or difference in social status are not emphasised – rather, they suggest, our shared individual, *emotional* responses make us 'ordinary'.

Ellis's argument (above) about the end of scarcity in broadcasting challenges cultural producers of all kinds, including TV producers, and all kinds of museum curators: there are (thanks to new technology) now many more sources of (conflicting) historical account and the position of elite producers as *the* experts, whether on history or anything else, is, at the very least, rendered less powerful, if not actually undermined. In this way technological developments, particularly the development and spread of digital technologies, have contributed to the destabilisation of the authority of the expert's (curator/producer) account of the world. However, while the existence of a range of accounts may signal an end of scarcity as Ellis argues (2000), the question of exactly how such accounts are mediated is of crucial importance. If the expert account carries more force, or if the non-expert is only represented in particular ways (and not others), then this directly impacts upon the weight that is ultimately given to accounts from different quarters. Harrison and Wessels are among several scholars who are arguing for a concept of public service *communication* to replace that of public service *broadcasting:*

> New forms of audience engagement exist, which should not be viewed as audience fragmentation but audience discernment constituted through an environment which is pluralistic, engaging, associative and critical: an environment that itself helps to stimulate the expression of a pluralism defined by the activities of diverse individuals and groups within their different social, cultural and political experiences and settings.
>
> (2005, p. 837)

Notice the absence of the national in the list of relevant 'experiences and settings'. The relevance and irrelevance of the notion of the national as a key reference point for the production and display of representation of so-called ordinary people continues to be vexed and is of course tied to governmental agendas as well as to commercial developments. The UK example is instructive; at least some of the issues arising in this country are likely to exist in other nation states where governments have pursued similar political and economic policies in recent times.

Political and economic contexts: the UK case

The idea of public culture as something which should be available as a proper part of the lives of all of the public was never straightforward and always begged questions of who constituted that public and how best it could be represented, as we have seen in the preceding discussion. However, with the coming to power of the Conservative Party in the 1980s, the idea itself came under severe attack. This attack extended to all institutions whose remit was the provision of publicly funded culture, including, of course, museums and public service broadcasting. Media histories observe that the period of deregulation and privatisation ushered in by the Conservative governments of 1979–97 in Britain inculcated a challenge to the very idea of the value of public service broadcasting. As Sussman summarises,

In the 1980s, the Thatcher and Reagan governments came to power with a mission to demolish the welfare state, discipline the working classes, and return regulatory power to the market. Conservatives in Britain savaged the media and its unions, first freezing though ultimately failing to eliminate the licensing fee provisions of the British Broadcasting Corporation (BBC)

(2003, p. 111)

Walsh makes a case for linking the politics of the New Right with the ideas of a 'post modern condition', whereby individualism reigns and there is, in Thatcher's notorious phrase, 'no such thing as society'. In terms of cultural policy, this meant New Right governments setting about dismantling, or at least reducing, the welfare state and attacking and reducing the power of local government. Proponents of New Right philosophy did not see cultural and educational activities as a citizen's right. The market was brought to bear on cultural institutions and, for example, entrance charges were introduced in public museums, which had previously been free as public services. Museums now competed as institutions in a global leisure market (Urry, 1996, p. 62).

Since the election of the New Labour government in 1997, the question of the social utility of culture has been a key policy concern. The contemporary incarnation of the continuing debate over the value and role of particular representations of the so-called 'ordinary person' sheds light also on what Mayo has described as the 'return of community', in which self-representation became tightly articulated with a governmental emphasis on locally based 'community' initiatives across areas such as cultural policy or neighbourhood regeneration (Mayo, 2006). Contemporary institutional discourses of participatory community are part of what has been called the Post-Washington Consensus, wherein policies of the New Right were followed by attempts by the Clinton and Blair administrations to temper the free reign of the market in some areas of life. (See pages 26–7 for a fuller discussion of the Post-Washington Consensus.)

Since the election of the Conservative-Liberal coalition government in 2010, a fast (and familiar) programme of attacks on the public sector is being proposed and enacted, justified by reference to the global economic crisis and the inability of the country to afford the existing public sector. As a core part of this emerging programme of cuts, the cultural sector is unsurprisingly coming under attack and here we witness a very different view, to that seen under New Labour, of the role of cultural production and cultural activity and a reconfiguring of what culture is. And yet UK Prime Minister David Cameron's 'Big Society' resorts to the same rhetorical territory of 'ordinary people', 'community' and 'voice', which we have seen growing in our story about the representation of the self since the nineteenth century. To understand this requires taking into account the now long-standing ideas associated with neo-liberalism.

It is widely accepted that neo-liberalism has achieved normative status. Hall notes that its big achievement in the UK is that it became society's 'common sense' (Davison et al., 2010, p. 27). Meanwhile scholars observe the paradox of proliferating self-representation and 'democratic deficit'; Turner writes of a 'demotic' turn in media, while Couldry observes that the idea of voice, specifically, is used in a particular and entirely undemocratic way in the globally entrenched political and economic philosophy of neo-liberalism (Couldry, 2010; Turner, 2010). Thus the proliferation of self-representation takes place as actual democratic opportunities for speaking and, crucially, for being heard are dramatically reduced. What can we make of self-representations, then, other than to dismiss them as largely undemocratic?

Conclusion: mediation and self-representation

For Ellis, the role of public service broadcasting (and we can apply this to cultural institutions in general) becomes one of facilitating the public in understanding the society in which we all live:

> No longer the agent of a standardizing notion of national unity, public service broadcasting can provide the forum within which the emerging culture of multiple identities can negotiate its antagonisms. This is in many ways the opposite of its former role: instead of providing displays of national unity, it deals in displays of national disunity, the better to bring about ways of resolving them.
>
> (2000, p. 87)

Raboy agrees that new formations of self-representations and group affiliations provoke crucial questions for the institutions of national public service broadcasting:

> locally, and irrespective of national borders, people will continue to create their own means of communication using whatever is available for the purpose. New transnational, even global media are emerging. What can one mean by public communication in this context?
>
> (2008, p. 363)

He further notes: 'The primary purpose of a public broadcaster is to do what no other mainstream media institution can be expected to do, and that is: put aside the interests of the state and commercial investors and work to promote democratic practices' (2008, p. 364). In this book I explore the suggestion that the notion of promoting democratic practices in media is not (only) an abstract idea. I show that to understand the overwhelming array of mediated self-representations by ordinary people in today's global media and cultural spaces, we need to deploy *mediation* as an analytical concept. There are explicit political differences between different kinds of mediated self-representation. Moreover, there are, as with the rest of media representations, many contradictions: ordinariness appears liberatory, progressive and, at the same time, cheap and reactionary, just as in earlier debates.

A key difference to today as compared with the history we have discussed is the digitally enabled proliferation of self-representations. But we cannot assume *a priori* what the digital capabilities mean; we need to ask on a case-by-case basis. Moreover we should not think that technological developments are the only thing distinguishing ordinary self-representations today from those produced in previous eras. We must remember the social, cultural and political contexts in which that technology is both used and developed. Thus we urgently need the tools to explore critically the kinds of ordinariness, the kinds of self-representation that surround us and that we participate in – as well as never forgetting the vital question of who is, and who is not, joining in, as Jenkins notes in relation to YouTube,

> [It] teaches us that a participatory culture is not necessarily a diverse culture. As John McMuria has shown us, minorities

are grossly under-represented – at least among the most heavily viewed videos on YouTube, which still tend to come most often from white middle class males. If we want to see a more 'democratic' culture, we need to explore what mechanisms might encourage greater diversity in who participates, whose work gets seen, and what gets valued within the new participatory culture.

(Jenkins, 2007)

In other words we need to ask what kind of mediation is at work. And thus in the following chapter I elaborate three dimensions of mediation – institutional, textual and cultural – offering thereby a conceptual framework with which to apprehend the ubiquitous mediated self-representations that we now routinely encounter.

3
Mediation

Introduction

The concept of mediation enables us to make sense of now ubiquitous self-representations. This chapter is in two sections. Firstly, in a section on mediation, I propose that the concept can be deployed to make sense of self-representation in digital culture. I elaborate on three conceptually distinct dimensions of mediation process – institutional, textual and cultural – which are deployed in the analysis of self-representation in Chapters 4–6. Secondly, in a section on audiences, I argue that established (and highly contested) categories of audience and text remain important, and show how theoretical and empirical scholarship in the field of audience research exploring the relationship between production, texts and audiences led to the concept of mediation.

The question of how to greet rapid developments in media and communications technologies, and coterminous cultural developments, sparks heated debate in the scholarly fields concerned. Recently writing by William Merrin and by David Gauntlett prompted a discussion as to whether, put crudely, the theories and methods developed in media studies education over the last several decades are in need of radical overhaul in the face of Web 2.0 – the internet 'generation' in which technological developments have enabled collaboration and participation on an unprecedented scale (e.g. Gauntlett, 2007, 2009; Merrin, 2008; and see also all of the articles published in Interactions 1 (1)). Thus Gauntlett argued that the concept of a Media Studies 2.0 indicates

> A corresponding recognition that the separate categories of 'producer' and 'audience' are collapsing, as a growing number of people become creators, arrangers and remixers of digital media.
>
> (Gauntlett, 2009, p. 149)

Indeed the very role of teachers and researchers of media and communication has been called into question because we are seen to be in an age when you can 'do it yourself', thus Joke Hermes argues,

> The moment audiences are producers and co-creators, as a 2.0 perspective suggests, they hardly need the mediating voice of research to tell them how what they are doing has meaning.
>
> (2009, p. 111)

The debate about a Media Studies 2.0 revolves in part around the idea that unmediated self-representation is, if not actually possible, at least a commonly held ideal, that is that it should be possible to 'speak for oneself' without being mediated by media producers, museum curators, academic researchers or other professionals. Indeed the idea that unmediated self-representation is conceivable also implies that technology and form do not play too important a role in shaping the meaning of a representation. Finally the ideal of unmediated self-representation downplays the ways in which people inevitably mediate their own representation by bringing to bear certain assumptions, attitudes and understandings of what a self-representation addressed to an audience should entail.

The contention that unmediated self-representation is possible, it seems to me, exists in all circles today (policy, media, academy, daily life) to the extent that such a *promise* now qualifies as common sense, while opportunities for its fulfilment apparently abound. There is a paradox here which is this: it is imagined to be possible to articulate, and subsequently to represent, an unmediated individual, 'true' self at precisely a time when the very idea of a unitary, fixed self has been widely and convincingly problematised in theory (e.g. Abercrombie and Longhurst, 1998; Butler, 1990; Hall, 1996). Moreover this promise of unmediated self-representation takes place in a context in which media scholars are emphasising precisely the question of how processes of mediation shape meaning – a context which Sonia Livingstone has referred to with the phrase 'the mediation of everything' (Livingstone, 2009). Self-representation is taking place across all kinds of media and cultural spaces at a time when it is widely acknowledged that there can be no self without mediation.

Mediation

We can identify four debates, which take the notion of mediation in different, although absolutely not exclusive, directions. Complicating any typology is the fact that, as Livingstone, Couldry and others have noted, the terms 'mediation' and 'mediatisation' have been used differently, and sometimes in overlapping ways, in diverse academic and linguistic traditions (e.g. Couldry, 2008; Livingstone, 2009). Having said that, all of the senses of mediation that I shall now introduce have a bearing on how the idea of mediation is used in this book. Firstly, the term 'mediation' has long been used to focus on the role of technology in meaning-making. More than 15 years ago, John Thompson used the term 'mediation' specifically to distinguish the communication that takes place via technology from the face-to-face interactions, which are not mediated by technology. He introduced a second term 'mediatisation' to refer to the more fundamental changes brought to bear in societies as a result of technical innovations (Thompson, 1995). More recently, Leah Lievrouw also uses the term 'mediation' to speak about research that is concerned in various ways with technological developments (Lievrouw, 2009). Observing that two sub-fields have structured US communication studies since its inception (namely, interpersonal communication and mass communication), she suggests that, while the relationship between these two areas has long been the subject of research, the development of digital media technologies has intensified their interconnection. Lievrouw proposes that the concept of mediation 'bridges' the two domains:

> I suggest that the concept of mediation, advanced as a bridge between the two traditions since the early days of new media research in the 1970s and 1980s, and further elaborated since the 1990s, may offer a promising direction for a discipline that

faces the challenge of reconceptualising communicative practices, technologies and social arrangements as inseparable, mutually-determining aspects of the communication process.

(Lievrouw, 2009, p. 304)

Jay David Bolter and Richard Grusin also emphasise a technological understanding of the concept of mediation, with their notion of remediation's twin logics of immediacy and hypermediacy:

Older electronic and print media are seeking to reaffirm their status within our culture as digital media challenge that status. Both new and old media are invoking the twin logics of immediacy and hypermediacy in their efforts to remake themselves and each other.

(Bolter and Grusin, 1999, p. 5)

The Mediatized Stories Network's[1] particular focus on the activity of digital storytelling is another example of a technological emphasis in the use of the term 'mediation'. In general we can summarise that scholarship concerned with the particular kinds of constraints, possibilities and social and cultural processes engendered by new media forms, deploys the concept of mediation in this technological sense. Moreover, in a period of intense debate about the potential of new media technologies to bring about massive changes to both social and political life, ideas about technology, as well as the technologies themselves, are central to how we understand the concept of mediation. In this book the term 'mediation' is used to emphasise technology – quite simply because technology intervenes in face-to-face interaction in all of the empirical examples discussed in the following chapters. The imagined, the actual, the hoped for outcomes of new technologies, as well as the fears they invoke and the difficulties they pose, I suggest, all play a role in the mediation of self-representation and therefore mediation – in the sense of technological mediation – is an underlying theme in the following chapters, and one to which I return in Chapter 7.

Secondly, the term 'mediation' is used to indicate a focus on the broader cultural context within which media meanings are made, remade and circulated. Livingstone suggests this theoretical development has been widely adopted:

It seems that we have moved from a social analysis in which the mass media comprise one among many influential but independent institutions whose relations with the media can be usefully analyzed to a social analysis in which everything is mediated, the consequence being that all influential institutions in society have themselves been transformed, reconstituted, by contemporary processes of mediation.

(Livingstone, 2009, p. 2)

Within a broad social analysis (to use Livingstone's phrase) debate rages over where the emphasis should lie. Silverstone called on the concept of processes of mediation to focus on the never-ending circulation of meaning that he suggests takes place. Silverstone (1999, 2005) placed the media (in their many guises) at the centre of these circulations, so that for him, the media are central to how and what we know. In this way, the centrality of the media to mediation forms part of an argument about why we should study the media (Silverstone, 1999). On the other hand, some authors use the notion of mediation to propose a radical decentring of the media (Couldry, 2006; Martin-Barbero, 1993). For Martin-Barbero, for example, the media are only one site – albeit an important one – through which meanings are generated and circulated; media are decentralised as the focus of media and cultural studies and the focus is now on daily life and 'mediations'. Martin-Barbero writes,

This is how communications began to be seen more as a process of mediations than of media, a question of culture and, therefore, not just a matter of cognitions but of re-cognition.

(1993, p. 2)

The research discussed in this book began by situating the media as absolutely central to the production of meaning in society, an approach exemplified by Silverstone's use of the term 'mediation'. In this way, self-representation was initially approached through in-depth study of the production processes of particular cases (Thumim, 2007). However this media-centred view was troubled by the empirical research in which some of the participants in projects that invited self-representation were offhand about the chances of their pieces appearing on public media and museum platforms.

These people were taking part much more for the group activity involved in the process than because of any perceived opportunity that they would eventually appear 'in the media'. This finding made clear that the centrality of media and cultural institutions in the lives of those representing themselves can never be assumed, but rather is always an empirical question. Despite this finding, the same empirical research confirmed that fundamentally unequal power relations exist between the cultural institutions and industries inviting or facilitating self-representation and the audiences taking up the opportunity (see Couldry, 2000a; Thumim, 2007). Mediation in this second sense of usage, then, is about the cultural processes which intervene in the circulation of meaning, but the extent to which the media are centred (Silverstone's view) or decentred (Martin-Barbero's view) in these processes is a question for empirical research and completely dependent on context. The understanding of mediation as the circulation of meaning provides the context to a narrower usage which focuses on representation – this is the third sense in which the concept of mediation is used, to which I now turn.

The third sense in which the concept of mediation is deployed is that which describes close readings of the processes (techniques, technologies, ideologies) which shape a representation that is produced and displayed in the media. In this sense, mediation is about the processes that must come between those represented in a particular media text and their audiences. Thus, for example, a member of the audience has decided to apply to take part in the *Capture Wales* digital storytelling project that she has seen advertised in her local library. Her digital story – the self-representation – comes about through workshop processes, conversations, technological affordances and limitations, institutional requirements and expectations, personal ideas about production and more besides. These are all examples of the processes of mediation shaping the self-representation which the woman in question ends up completing. This third sense of mediation has long been used in media and film studies work about representation and particularly in research addressing the documentary and other representations of 'the real'. Such scholarship has explored questions like how the representation is put together, what it focuses on, what tone is used, what it looks like, what is excluded and so on. This use of the concept of mediation has entailed a focus on production and editing, asking, for example, how production values and editing styles and conventions *mediate* the real (e.g. Corner, 1994). This sense of mediation speaks very directly to the question of *how* members of the public are representing themselves in the array of platforms available in digital culture on- and offline? That is to say, how do the platforms, their particular styles and conventions mediate the self-representation of participants?

The fourth sense of the term 'mediation' is used, for example, by Elihu Katz in his focus on the question of *who* it is that mediates. Over 20 years ago, Katz referred to the idea of 'disintermediation' and explored the suggestion that members of the public might nowadays communicate with each other without media professionals as intermediaries (Katz, 1988, pp. 30–1). The empirical work presented in Chapters 4–6, combined with the historical view of self-representation offered in Chapter 2, suggests that rather than an undoing of mediation, as is implied in the term 'disintermediation', there might well be new intermediaries taking up a position between producers of self-representations and their audiences. Preliminary findings from an ongoing research project about local media ecology in the city of Leeds, UK, support these findings, suggesting that key individuals play an extremely important role in mediating the circulation of news in the local media ecology.[2] For example, Emma Bearman, who runs a very well-known news and culture website publishing pieces by members of the public pertaining to all aspects of arts and culture news and events in the city of Leeds[3] plays the role of mediator between different parts of the media ecology in the city. Similarly, Mike Chitty is a community activist and development worker who has a blog and is active in a number of social networking sites and online spaces relevant to Leeds. Chitty republishes, circulates and comments on news and opinion. In this way he can be seen as a mediator between particular communities, more traditional news media and wider publics.[4] Research thus suggests that while media professionals may not always play the role of intermediary, nevertheless we are not seeing a process of disintermediation, rather we are seeing a process by which the role of intermediary is played by media professionals and other kinds of leader; intermediaries remain *vitally* important.

I have explored the four senses in which the term 'mediation' is used in media and communications scholarship. Firstly, I introduced research which deploys the term 'mediation' to focus on the role of technological developments as mediators of meanings in society.

Secondly, I discussed the debates which use the term 'mediation' to indicate an interest in the circulation of meaning within cultural contexts; I noted that scholars take different positions in these debates regarding the extent to which the media institutions and technologies should be seen as playing a central role in such processes. The third sense of the term 'mediation' that I identified in the scholarship appears in work which uses the term to refer to analysis of exactly how representations are constructed – in particular, representations of the real. I noted that such work includes textual analysis as well as attention to how processes of production shape representations. The final use of the term 'mediation' that I explored is where the term is used in considering the ways in which changes in digital culture may herald a weakening, or at the very least a change, in the way in which key people themselves function as mediators. I reiterate that these four ways of deploying the term 'mediation' are not exclusive. Indeed these four areas of usage often overlap in the scholarship which uses this key concept. What is clear from this brief overview of the scholarly uses of 'mediation' in the fields of media and communication studies is that unmediated representation is never possible and, moreover, in the age of digital culture, the *processes* of mediation themselves require analytical attention, perhaps more than before.

Mediation as bridge

In 2000 Fornäs argued that mediation was a crucial concept in media and cultural studies for balancing the analysis of texts with the analysis of lived experience, rather than opting for one or the other (Fornäs, 2000). Thus, for Fornäs, the concept of mediation precisely links the second and third areas of usage that I have introduced above. More recently scholars have described mediation as a bridge (e.g. Fornäs, 2008; Lievrouw, 2009). The idea of mediation as a bridge reminds us of the everyday meaning of the term in situations of dispute resolution. But mediation as a bridge also invokes the ways in which the concept has come to be used in different ways by scholars across the fields of media, communication and cultural studies (see my discussion in the previous section) and emphasises the overlaps between these different uses of the term. The concept of mediation will not resolve all debate in the field (and nor should we expect it to) but it does foreground processes of debate and processes of meaning-making. Indeed I suggest that the concept of mediation as a bridge invokes the range of quite different debates discussed above as well as the links between them. Further, mediation recalls Hall's notion of negotiation, posited in his 1973 Encoding/Decoding paper. Encoding/decoding is discussed in the overview of audience research to which I will turn below.

In her discussion of the increasingly prevalent concept of mediation, Livingstone notes that Raymond Williams (1977, p. 100)

> remained dissatisfied with the notion of mediation, noting that mediation, like reflection, still assumes a fundamental and problematic distinction between (rather than mutually constitutive relation between) the representation and that which is represented.
>
> (Livingstone, 2009, p. 14, note 15)

Williams (1977) points to a problem inherent in the idea of representation, but it is not a problem we can avoid by eschewing either the concept of representation or that of mediation. I suggest that 'mediation' has come to be used in contemporary scholarship precisely to draw attention to the '... mutually constitutive relation between) the representation and that which is represented'. The concept of mediation focuses our analyses on processes in between representations and reality, whether at macro or micro level, and in so doing foregrounds the mutual construction (of representation and reality) to which Williams referred.

The conceptual space delineated by the notion of mediation builds on this history of research that aimed to think about meaning being made relationally, involving production and reception as well as texts. Taken together, all of this work suggests that to understand meaning-making – and therefore power relations – both the detail of specific instances of production, text and reception, and the broader social contexts of media use should at the very least be acknowledged as part of the processes of mediation. In this perspective, the notion of mediation delineates a specific form of enquiry, which stresses both the multiple factors that shape meaning (construct it) and the open-ended nature of meaning-making. I now turn to the ways in which the notion of mediation is deployed in the empirical analyses presented in subsequent chapters, exploring self-representation in digital culture as always and unavoidably mediated.

Dimensions of mediation: institutional, textual and cultural processes

The focus of the analysis in the following chapters is on the interaction between production, text and audience, in particular instances where the reception context is altered because the audience member has (albeit temporarily) become a producer. These interactions and the resultant self-representations are all subject to processes of mediation. While acknowledging that these processes are ultimately endless (cf. Silverstone 1999, 2005), I explore some specific moments in the process of mediation. The focus is on three dimensions of mediation: *institutional mediation, cultural mediation* and *textual mediation*. This is not to suggest that mediation is in practice separated in this way, nor that these dimensions describe every kind of mediation at work, but simply that such a breakdown is conceptually useful in order to take us beyond the amorphous idea that everything is mediated and to explore what this means in relation to specific examples.

In the conceptual separation of processes of mediation into three dimensions, I build on the work that has taken account of producers, texts and audiences/reception discussed below. I suggest that the concepts of production, text and reception map onto the concepts of *processes of institutional mediation, processes of textual mediation* and *processes of cultural mediation*. These conceptual changes contribute to the development of the theoretical approach, as I shall now explain. I develop the argument for a focus on processes of mediation above. Next, I suggest a move away from the terms 'producers' and 'audiences', because this division becomes confusing when the focus is on one among several ways in which members of the audience have begun to participate in production. Further, the term 'institutional mediation' is both broader and more specific than either of the terms 'producers' or 'production'. The concept of processes of institutional mediation specifically points to the production contexts of the media industries – whether that is a public service institution like the BBC or a commercial company like Facebook. At the same time, the term 'institution' is broad enough to allow us to group together discussion of the individual persons directly working on producing self-representations with/by members of the public, with those many others in the institutions and related bodies, such as funders and partner organisations, who have a bearing on the outcome without actually being involved in the day-to-day running of particular programmes and projects.

I refer to 'processes of cultural mediation' to describe the processes of mediation that have to do with how the points of view and experience of the audience members who participate by producing their self-representations shape the resultant self-representations. I move from the term 'audience', or 'reception', to the concept of processes of cultural mediation because 'the audience' as a term does not adequately describe the people in question – the audience member temporarily engaged in production – and certainly the term 'reception' does not describe the type of audience activity with which we are concerned here. The concept of processes of cultural mediation is used to indicate the focus on what the audience/participants bring to the production of self-representation in terms of abilities, expectations, understandings – what is brought to the mediation process from the participants who are outside the institution. But cultural mediation also invokes Martin-Barbero, Couldry and Silverstone and the questioning of the place of media in daily lives.

The notion of process of cultural mediation to refer to the mediation processes that emanate from the activity of audience members engaged in production is a specific and purposeful use of the term 'culture', which does not intend to deny that cultural formations shape all aspects of the mediation process. For example, the cultural formations of the institutional employees are clearly also important. Nevertheless, the separation of the mediation process into processes of 'institutional' and 'cultural mediation' is a useful working model.

Finally, I suggest that we retain the word 'text' in the term 'processes of textual mediation'. The idea of *processes* of textual mediation enables us to take on board the long-standing criticisms levelled at the project of textual analysis (see, for example, Couldry, 2000b; Morley, 2006) and at the same time to attend to matters of textual representation. Recent work by Buckingham highlights the importance of the text. In a critique of the *use of* data from 'visual research', he makes two vital points:

> Analysis needs to address the 'affordances' of different modes of representation (drawings, photography, or video, for example),

but it should also address the social meanings that attach to these modes, and the social expectations that surround them.
(Buckingham, 2009, p. 648)

In these assertions Buckingham takes as given the idea that if representation takes place, then mediation is unavoidable. Let's take the social networking website Facebook as an example; the implication of the two points Buckingham makes is that we must ask how the practice of using a photograph on one's profile picture on Facebook shapes the kind of representation that is possible. What does photography afford in this setting? Equally what does the decision to upload a drawing instead of a standard self-portrait mean – what does the mode of a pencil drawing afford the person representing him or herself? – which is *different to what a photograph allows*. Moreover, Buckingham is making the point that the photography and pencil drawing (in my Facebook example) are not neutral modes of representation but rather they invoke social expectations both for the person making the representation and for the consumers of the representation. In choosing to represent oneself on Facebook with a quirky pencil drawing, what is one conveying about oneself and what will imagined and actual audiences make of such a mode of representation? While acknowledging debate about the relevance and authority of textual analysis today, I argue that analysis of texts is a crucial aspect of understanding how self-representations are mediated in digital culture – that is as long as the texts are explored in relation to the context in which they are produced. In this study the texts are explored in relation to institutional and cultural processes of mediation.

Let me now illustrate how the three dimensions of mediation process are deployed in the following chapters. Firstly, how are the self-representations of the people who participate mediated either by an institutional invitation to tell their story or by the fact that they must represent themselves textually in order to be part of online social networks? For example, *Capture Wales* took place within BBC Wales and there were a range of stakeholders in that organisation for whom the invitation to self-representation existed for different reasons. Thus, for members of the team that ran *Capture Wales*, the project provided an opportunity for people to represent themselves truthfully, as opposed to being inadequately represented by media professionals. This view shaped how the team ran the workshops, advised the participants and assisted in the production of self-representations, as well as shaping the form that the representations took. On the other hand, for senior management in the BBC, *Capture Wales* was a successful project because participants came away with a positive attitude to, and even a sense of ownership of, the BBC, which in turn reinforced the legitimacy of this institution. These views of the role of *Capture Wales* determined the funding and internal support that the project received. For the BBC's middle management, however, the role of self-representation was often unclear and this led to the *Capture Wales* production team facing difficulties in finding broadcast spaces to exhibit the self-representations to a wider public. I argue that there were tensions between these varied views on the meaning and purpose of self-representations. Further, these tensions shaped the resultant texts and are part of what constituted institutional mediation in *Capture Wales*. The question of institutional mediation is explored through a range of examples including *Capture Wales, Faking It*, The Smithsonian Institute and Facebook, in the following chapters on broadcasters, museum and art worlds, and self-representation online.

Secondly, how are the self-representations mediated by the making and display of the text? That is, how do the form and technologies used, as well as the location and presentation of the text, mediate the resultant self-representations? For example, a group of young people took part in the *London's Voices 16–19* project and their self-representations took the form of poems that they wrote in workshops run by a professional writer. These poems were typed up. Thumbnail titles on the *16–19* website were accompanied by a description of the workshop from which the poems came. The thumbnails are reached via the Museum of London homepage. That the Museum of London invited and facilitated these self-representations shows that the museum (and the funding body, the Heritage Lottery Fund) considers self-representation important; at the same time, the framing, which includes a description of the project, alerts the web user to what these texts are. In this way, it is clear that self-representation must be explained to an audience, so that the status of the material is clearly signposted for them as self-representations by young people produced under specific circumstances. These self-representations cannot be left to speak entirely for themselves. Such signposting and framing are examples of the processes of textual mediation explored in the following chapters.

Thirdly, how are the self-representations of the members of the public who participate shaped by their own cultural formations and the expectations that they bring to any act of participation? For example, how did a person's view of themselves, of the BBC and of their relation to the BBC shape what they expected to produce in the *Capture Wales* workshop and, subsequently, what they did produce? Participants' conception of themselves as both 'ordinary' and, at the same time, unique, leads to self-representations that both call upon, and at the same time undo, the idea of the ordinary, as is discussed in the previous chapter – or people's expectations of what a project is for may lead to changes in what is produced and how it is produced. One group of young people took part in *London's Voices 16–19* because, for example, of the opportunity it afforded them to learn photography. Yet this was not the main aim of the project from the point of view of the museum staff. The curators running the project had intended those groups doing photography projects to use disposable cameras in the interests of resources (time and funds) and also in the interests of maintaining equality between the different participating groups. But this particular group of young people worked with a professional photographer and the emphasis of the project moved to learning skills in photography. These are two examples of the processes of cultural mediation that are explored in the following chapters.

In practice, these dimensions of mediation are not separate. For instance, in the third example – *cultural mediation* – the textual possibilities, engendered by the use of professional instead of disposable cameras, shape the resultant self-representations just as much as the focus on learning photography does. Thus the processes of mediation that take place around this decision are in fact both textual and cultural ones. Nonetheless, for the purposes of analysis, it is useful to separate the dimensions of mediation in this way. The three dimensions of the processes of mediation are explored in relation to a range of examples of self-representation in the following three chapters on broadcasters, museum and art worlds, and self-representation online.

Audience research

Almost ten years ago Livingstone (2004) highlighted anxieties that existed in the field of audience studies with the question: what is the audience researcher to do in the age of the internet? As the preceding discussion highlights, research on media audiences must now take account of audience activity that today includes (for increasing numbers of the audience) representing themselves in media spaces. I am by no means suggesting that this activity, by what still remains a minority of the audience, has become more important than other kinds of audience activity. According to Dovey and Lister, opportunities for participation, collaboration and production online – and they refer not only to self-representation, but to all kinds of participation – are only taken up by the few:

> Web business builds on the 98 per cent: 2 per cent rule – 98 per cent of traffic will pass through the site whilst only 2 per cent will stay and get involved in the social network or other 'producerly' activities'.
>
> (2009, p. 142)

Nevertheless, self-representation *is* an activity with which audiences have increasing opportunities to engage and this observation suggests that exploring self-representation is now a necessary part of audience research.

The articles in Livingstone's edited volume on audiences and publics (Livingstone, 2005a) attest to the current interest in framing members of the public's participation as part of the inquiry into audiences. For example, Mehl notes,

> But the main programmes on the major channels today tend to be characterized by a concern to involve the audience and by the constant celebration of their proximity.
>
> (2005, p. 83)

While self-representation is, of course, not the only type of audience activity or the only type of audience involvement, nevertheless it is one which demands attention as part of the study of what it is that audiences do. Self-representation demands attention because of the ways in which it has come to be both a part of what audiences do and a part of what media and cultural institutions deliberately foster. This does raise the problem of whether the single concept of audience can contain the range of activities we are asking of it (see, for example, Livingstone, 2004). I suggest that it is conceptually important to retain the concept of *audience* because doing so positions participation and self-representation *as a part of* what it is that people who are in the audience nowadays do. If we retain the concept of *audience*, it follows that the history of research on the engagement and activity of audiences is the key to an analysis of the contemporary activity of self-representation.

All of the research in media and communications and related fields has always invoked some idea of the audience – and it continues to do so. The study of media and culture has been approached from a range of very different perspectives across the social sciences and arts, as Boyd-Barrett and Newbold note, 'the field is a term which enables us to discuss under one umbrella the eclectic nature of mass communications research' (1995). One influential concept of the field of media studies is Lazarsfelds's division between two traditions: the administrative and the critical (Lazarsfeld, 1941). This distinction divided research which was carried out to address the concerns of public and private bodies, for instance policy-orientated research, from that which sought critical and theoretical understandings of media and communications for the sake of scholarly endeavour and social critique. In fact, this division itself should be understood as located in a particular historical moment and location – the early days of media and communications research in the USA (e.g. Hardt, 1992). The division between administrative and critical approaches refers to media studies within the social sciences. As Corner notes, media studies, at least in Britain, drew on the arts as well as the social sciences disciplines (Corner, 1995b). However, across the various divisions in the field(s), some idea of the audience was always invoked in early research, whether that research offered critical analysis of films, surveys of public opinion or experiments which directly addressed anxieties about media effects.

Studies of effects in what is known as the media effects tradition addressed societal and governmental concerns with the possible effects of media on its audience (Gerbner, 1995 (1969); Katz and

Lazarsfeld, 1955). Writings by members of the Frankfurt School addressed and sought to expose the ideological operations of media on the audience as 'mass' (see, for example, Adorno and Horkheimer, 1993 (1944)). Early textual criticism drew on models from literary studies, particularly structuralism and semiotics to 'read' the messages of media texts (see, for example, Barthes, 1973 [1957]; Eco, 1981; Hall, 1973; Wright, 1975); in this work, the critic or the semiotician had the skills to 'read' the text and to decipher, for example, the dominant ideological message.

This extremely limited and thus necessarily crude characterisation of the history of what has always been an extremely diverse field of study serves to indicate that early work from the range of approaches to the study of media and communication placed emphasis on the power of media institutions and their productions to have some kind of impact, effect or consequence for the lives of their audience, even where the research is not in the particular tradition of media effects research. Thus we can summarise that assumptions, and frequently concern, about the audience-informed approaches to the study of media from their beginnings – even when those studies were not framed as being explicitly concerned with the audience.[5]

Over time the fields of communication studies, media studies, cultural studies and film studies have seen developments of, and challenges to, the approaches of earlier work (including subsequent studies by the authors of the earlier work). Of particular importance was the challenge to the implicit conception of the audience as passive recipients of messages – a view underpinning so much of the earlier study in the field. For example, the proponents of the 'uses and gratifications' approach asked what audiences got out of media texts that they consumed, thus moving the focus to exploring *how* audiences consumed media (see, for example, Katz, Blumler and Gurevitch, 1974). Around the same time the notion of polysemy was developed in the field of semiotics (Eco, 1981; Hall, 1973). In his seminal article, 'Encoding and decoding in the television discourse', Hall drew on ideas from semiotics to develop the concepts of encoding and decoding, and the notions of preferred, oppositional and negotiated decodings of TV texts. 'Encoding and decoding in the television discourse' remains important because, in that model, Hall emphasised the importance of sites of production, text and reception as all contributing to the *production of media meanings*. Moreover, he emphasised the processes of meaning-making between such sites. The period following the publication of the Hall's article saw a wealth of studies that explored the processes of reception. The suggestion that meaning is both constructed and varied meant that investigating the audience empirically came to be seen as central to understanding what (and how) media mean (see, for example, Liebes and Katz, 1990; Livingstone, 1998; Morley, 1980). Critics of this approach argued that the emphasis on the (semiotically) *active audience* led to over-optimistic interpretations of audience power and, consequently, insufficient attention was given to the unequal power relations between media institutions and their audiences (see, for example, Seaman, 1992). The useful implication that I take from the critiques of audience studies, and the notion of the active audience, is the necessity to consider the meanings audiences make *always in relation to* the producing institutions, as well as to specific texts.

A further critique of audience studies was articulated in Ien Ang's influential observation that 'the audience' does not actually exist but instead is constructed by academics and the media industry and in the interests of market research to describe people for particular purposes (Ang, 1990). This means that researching social subjects as if they were solely members of the audience for a specific programme is seen as a failure to grasp the complexity of people's lives. Critics have suggested that the focus on the reception of particular programmes, for example, fails to account for the place of a range of media in people's daily lives and indeed the possibility that the media are not always and inevitably of central importance. The ethnographic turn in media studies moved to focus on the relations between media and daily life (e.g. Martin-Barbero, 1993; Silverstone, 1994; Silverstone and Hirsch, 1992).

The development of ethnographic work in media studies also criticised the view of the audience as 'reader' and of media productions as 'texts' akin to written texts and their readers. The argument suggests that understanding media outputs as texts fails to address the different ways in which media are consumed, lived with or even ignored by audiences (Morley, 2006). Thus more recent work on media audiences has increasingly seen audiences as diffused, embedded and contextualised – often radically so to the point where the very category 'audience' is regarded as limited (see Abercrombie and Longhurst,

1998, for a useful summary). Taken together, these critiques of uses of the category 'audience', and of the focus on audience 'readings' of media as 'texts', suggest that it would be wise to guard against reifying the category 'audience', or indeed that of 'text'. Instead research should continue to look empirically at what particular audiences are doing, in relation to specific texts and specific production contexts.

Hall develops the ideas first posited in the article 'Encoding and decoding in the television discourse' (Hall, 1973) in a later work with Paul Du Gay in which they note,

> Where is meaning produced? Our 'circuit of culture' suggests that, in fact, meanings are produced at several different sites and circulated through several different processes or practices (the cultural circuit).... Meaning is constantly being produced and exchanged in every personal and social interaction in which we take part.... It is also produced in a variety of different media...
>
> (Hall 1997, p. 3)

The idea of the 'circuit of culture' suggests that, if we still want to consider the meaning of a certain kind of media production, then we should attend not only to producers, texts and audiences, but also to *the spaces in between*. At least in relation to 'old media', it is now widely agreed that meaning is not fixed by producers in texts, rather it is made and remade in the processes of production and in reception contexts. Firstly, producers of media content might have optimistic views of how their programme will be understood, but they cannot control what it will mean for viewers. More contentiously, it is widely recognised, across the many disciplinary areas that contribute to media and communication studies, that content varies widely and should be examined in and for itself, rather than being treated, for example, as a stimulus with which to investigate the audience (see, for example, Corner, 1999; Livingstone, 2004). Theoretical developments concerned with the ways in which meanings are produced thus highlighted the importance of analysis of texts, audience and production, in this way developing theories of representation, reception and production.

The turn that audience research was taking in the 1980s included several empirical responses to the theoretical idea (articulated in Hall's encoding/decoding model) that meaning is made in sites of production, text and reception *and in the processes* that link these sites. For example, Buckingham's case study of the British soap opera *Eastenders*, Corner, Richardson and Fenton's reception study about TV communication of the nuclear energy issue, D'Acci's case study of the US drama series *Cagney and Lacey*, and Hobson's case study of the British soap opera *Crossroads* have in common their attention to some combination of contexts of production, analysis of texts and investigation of reception. That is not to say that equal weight is given to all of these areas in each of these studies; for instance, the emphasis in Corner et al.'s study is on the reception of the programmes, but the way that a range of programmes depict the issue is understood to be important:

> Thus, the research, rather than holding the idea of 'television' constant in order to explore response, would also explore variables both in the rhetorical intentions and discursive operation of sample programmes.
>
> (1990, p. 9)

The context in which these programmes were produced does not form part of the empirical work presented in Corner et al.'s study (although these contexts are alluded to and therefore are taken into account); rather, the research is about the reception of particular examples of texts. D'Acci's study of *Cagney and Lacey* and Buckingham's study of *EastEnders* both look at production, texts and reception, and explore how the meaning of the programmes is made and remade in these moments and locations. The approach in all of these research examples highlights the question of *how* it is that meaning is produced in production context, audience response and the formal aspects of texts. These earlier works are suggestive for understanding contemporary self-representation through the concept of mediation.

Livingstone sounded a cautionary note in 2004 when she observed that scholarship about 'new' media has tended to ignore the insights about meaning-making that have been established in relation to 'old' media:

> We seem to treat 'the internet' as a 'black box', despite having developed a complex theory of codes, genre, mode of address etc for analysing television.
>
> (2004, p. 5)

In the following chapters I use the concept of mediation as a route to moving beyond 'treating "the internet" as a "black box"'. I show that this concept can be deployed to build on the theories of audience, texts and production in such a way as to be able to use them to understand the self-representations now routinely appearing across the platforms of both 'old' and 'new' media.

4
Broadcasters

Introduction

The routine appearance of opportunities for self-representation across spaces run by commercial and public service broadcasters begs the question – what is it that we are seeing? Ordinary people's participation in broadcast spaces has often been told as a story of extremes – between exploitative appearance and meaningful participation. In recent versions of this story we find critically lauded digital storytelling projects at one extreme and reality TV programmes at the other (e.g. Turner, 2010). Between the poles are a range of now-familiar practices such as the use of the amateur image and personal story in news and current affairs, the continued use of phone-ins and audience discussion programmes and indeed the use of personal testimony in 'serious' documentary. Self-representations by ordinary people sit within a very wide set of participatory activities in broadcast TV.[1]

In this chapter, the now concluded, award-winning *Capture Wales* digital storytelling project is taken as an exemplary case of self-representation in public service broadcasting. In spite of the fast-moving state of the digital culture in which contemporary broadcasters operate, and in which all sorts of projects and programmes, activities and applications come and go, digital storytelling (and often this UK PSB-run project in particular) is repeatedly explored in the most up-to-date international media and communications scholarship (e.g. Burgess, 2006; Burgess and Klaebe, 2009; Couldry, 2008; Hartley, 2008; Hartley and McWilliam, 2009; Meadows and Kidd,

2009; Turner, 2010; Wardle and Williams, 2008). In what follows, in-depth qualitative research on the processes of mediation-shaping self-representation in the BBC Wales' seven-year digital storytelling project (2001–8) is discussed in three parts – institutional, cultural and textual mediation.[2] The final part of the chapter considers the questions raised by this empirical work for our critical understanding of the role of self-representation in broadcasters' activities.

Broadcasters, self-representation and digital culture

We are not going to see the 'death of television' any time soon (e.g. Turner, 2010). While the international broadcast market is complex, varied and changing, as we advance through the second decade of the twenty-first century, TV remains culturally central. In the UK, for example,

> The public still consistently rates television as the communica-
> tions device they would most miss if it was taken away. In 2005 –
> 22% of 16–24 year olds said they would miss TV the most, and
> almost incredibly that has actually increased to 36% in the last
> year.
>
> (Richards, 2011)
>
> As for the type of device that people use to consume media, the
> television set was the most used device, with 90% of consumers
> saying they use it each day.
>
> (OFCOM, 2010, p. 33)

Statistics like these, which indicate the continued role of TV in people's lives, make clear that broadcast policy is of crucial importance in the age of digital culture, in particular for the survival of broadcast spaces with a public service remit. Scholars are grappling with the problem of what to call public service broadcasting in a digital cultural context. Some suggest a move from 'public service broadcasting' to 'public service communications' in order to encompass a range of activities by *broadcasters* that include but are not limited to *broadcasting* (e.g. Harrison and Wessels, 2005; Murdock, 2010; Raboy, 2008). Whatever language is used, we are seeing a renewed effort to argue for the retention of public service spaces within the sites deployed by broadcasters, which now include TV and internet platforms. Contemporary technological, political and economic environments are seen as offering both opportunity and threat to such public spaces (e.g. Flew and Cunningham, 2010). The more general debates about the role of public service broadcasting in a digital and multi-platform environment become focused in particular ways when we consider the audience activity of self-representation.

Almost 20 years ago, discussing the history of the Access idea in broadcasting, Corner noted,

> As television becomes increasingly open to market-driven channel choice in Britain, the survival of the very public space in which access has always had its difficult, marginalised existence is threatened. Within the new programme formulas, there will inevitably be a tendency for the accessed ordinary to be made productive within the terms of market competition.
>
> (1994, p. 33)

Indeed during, and since, the 1990s reality TV programmes have proliferated to the extent that such programming is probably the main location for self-representation in broadcast spaces.[3] In 'Making Class and Self Through Televised Ethical Scenarios', an Economic and Social Research Council funded project (2005–7) about reality TV audiences in the UK,[4] our research team counted how much reality TV programming was scheduled on free-to-view UK TV channels during one typical week – our conclusion was, unsurprisingly to anyone who watches TV, that the schedules were entirely dominated by this kind of programming. Scholars have developed the argument that members of the audience who participate in reality TV function as commodities in these programmes – producing wealth for the commercial TV stations and an audience for the public service broadcaster (Andrejevic, 2004; Turner, 2010). What I want to emphasise here is that one of the ways in which this commoditised audience appears in reality TV programmes is as textual self-representations embedded within programmes that have long been discussed in terms of genre hybridity (e.g. Hill, 2005). Thus, I suggest, we can begin to understand self-representation as a genre, found *and used*, in a range of contexts including, but not limited to, those in which a key function of the self-representing audience is indeed a commodity.

If it is the case that self-representations are *used* in quite different contexts, then the self-representation in broadcast spaces requires further attention. Dovey's comments in 2000 suggest that Corner's predictions (above) were correct:

> So much of contemporary factual television is based upon ordinary people's speech that it is easy to fall into the presumption that the airwaves are full of people 'speaking for themselves' when in fact they are saying what the script requires of them in the time the script requires to be filled, with all the attendant mediations of representational processes that go to shape their inputs.
>
> (Dovey, 2000, p. 110)

Dovey's call for analysis of the 'mediations of representational processes' is as urgent now as it was ten years ago – the airwaves remain 'full of people "speaking for themselves" ' – leading to the question – what makes this a self-representation? What is at stake 'behind the scenes' when an individual represents themselves? This is a question of processes and, I suggest, is best approached via the use of the analytical framework laid out in Chapter 2 – mediation processes of text, culture and institution. I turn now to explore these dimensions of mediation in relation to self-representation in BBC Wales' digital storytelling project, *Capture Wales*.

Capture Wales: textual mediation

In this section I focus on the processes of textual mediation that shape self representation in *Capture Wales*, raising speculative contrasts to, and similarities with, textual mediation of other examples of self-representation as I go along. Ellis neatly observed 'Any broadcast text is an assemblage of communicative attempts' (2010, p. 192). In looking at textual mediation we are asking what work these self-representations are doing. But, of course, we must also ask – what is it that we want them to do? As I suggested in Chapter 1, the idea of self-representation ultimately holds together two unlike discourses – that of therapy and that of democracy. The idea of self-representation is used to promise a more truthful account in order to address perceived absences in representation, misrepresentations and the idea that it is the representations made by others that are mediated, consequently indirect and intrinsically less truthful. But in promising truth, the idea of self-representation is also used to make a claim to authenticity and, in so doing, privileges the discourse of personal experience. A statement on the original *Capture Wales* site drew attention to the question of truth:

Are all the stories true?

We publish these stories in all good faith but, as Alys Lewis hints in her History or Mystery? story, it's sometimes difficult to tell where the border between fact and fiction lies.[5]

(*Capture Wales* website)

In *Capture Wales*, self-representations conform to the first-person experiential voice-over that is a defining feature of the digital storytelling form. And yet, as the above quotation signals, there is no certainty that what we are hearing is in fact truth. Here the self-representation form is one that explicitly allows that 'truth' is subjective and yet, paradoxically, the idea of self-representation promises a more truthful representation both for the person representing and for her audience.

In *Capture Wales* the very thing that was under construction, the 'ordinary person', was undermined as a possibility even as it was constructed, in this way highlighting the tension which accompanies any ascription of 'ordinary person'. For example, Dai Evans' digital story *My Two Families* played knowingly with the construction of the 'ordinary person'. After an introduction to himself and his family, photographs of green shop mannequins in strange poses are accompanied by a voice-over introducing a 'second family'. The story is amusing precisely because it parodies the audience's familiarity with the cliché of the 'ordinary' man. A particularly interesting feedback comment for the purposes of this discussion states,

I was intrigued by the title, but at first I thought it was going to be another (rather boring) family memoir; but Dai was full of surprises and his warm, wry, mischievous sense of humour came

across very effectively in the voiceover. Great pictures too! Nick
Passmore, Llandrindod Wells, Wales, February 2003.[6]

(*Capture Wales* website)

This comment undercuts the construction of the 'ordinary person'
suggesting that there is a recognisable genre – 'ordinary people'
speaking about family life and at the same time making clear that
the construction of the 'ordinary person' cannot hold and is not
what is interesting about people. The whole digital story is two
minutes long and sits on the website alongside many other individual self-representations, each of which destabilise the concept
of the 'ordinary person'. At the same time, the collection of these
stories highlights commonalities (as well as differences) between
members of the public and thus, in each digital story, as well as
in their collection and display on this website, the notion of the
'ordinary person' is reconstructed. This example from the *Capture
Wales* website suggests that the processes of textual mediation at work
here consisted of an interaction between producer and participant,
rather than, for example, a producer representation and a participant
resistance.

The *Capture Wales* digital stories are recognisable as digital stories
that have been produced by a BBC project. They are of a uniform
length (between two and three minutes). They all use first-person
voice-over and storytellers are encouraged to tell stories from a personal perspective or about a personal experience. They mostly use
still photographs and sometimes a very small amount of video. While
these digital stories are all made by different individuals, they share
characteristics that make them recognisable as digital stories produced by the *Capture Wales* project. They are considered and carefully
constructed. Creative Director Meadows describes them as 'multime-
dia sonnets from the people'. The voice-over is written in workshops
that begin with discussions, games and a 'storytelling circle' and
conclude with help with editing from expert tutors and finally the
recording of the voice-over with an expert sound recordist assisting.
The way that sound is used typically works to unite the stories as
Capture Wales digital stories and also as recognisably following in the
tradition of digital storytelling as set out by the Center for Digital
Storytelling in Berkeley, California.[7] The sound in these stories supports a poetic aesthetic. The *Capture Wales* digital stories generally

use family photographs, 'family archives', sometimes people's own drawing or artworks, and sometimes some video as well. Meadows uses the term 'scrapbook aesthetic' to describe the look of these stories, which are self-representations purposefully and clearly marked as constructed from the family albums of 'ordinary people', but carefully crafted, digitally reproduced and lingered over – suggesting a valuing of the memories on offer.[8]

The BBC claim to quality is signalled in the macro-texts of the websites and TV programmes by which the self-representations are framed. Here, quality is about the authority of the institution and this is indicated by a particular and serious, 'tasteful' institutional look to the website by the use of professional equipment and expertise for the individual stories (sound, writing, photography). Finally, this quality in the production process is intended to lead to a 'quality' outcome for the wider audience, as well as to provide satisfaction to those who participated. There is a tension over the designation of quality when this amateur aesthetic is employed between, for example, what might be seen as a 'bad photograph', or a story that is in 'bad taste', and the careful designation of the photograph or the narrative, as constituting a quality digital story in *Capture Wales*. This is the quality of amateur content – the best that self-representation can be made to be; but absolutely marked as such.

It is well established for reality TV programmes to include collage using old family photographs introducing participants, to-camera confidences and emotional interviews with loved ones delivering a familial and personal perspective. Recent examples include the UK's *X Factor* and *So You Think You Can Dance*. In analysing the data for the ESRC *Class and the Self* project about reality TV audiences, we found that to-camera moments were precisely those when the watching audience was most engaged – being prompted to talk either to the screen, each other or both. This is empirical evidence of something broadcasters know and also something that the longer history of self-representation in broadcasting tells us – that the mode of self-representation engages the audience (see Skeggs, Thumim and Wood, 2008).

In analysing the reality TV data (both text and audience reaction), we made the argument that participants are called on to represent themselves – that the rules of the genre of reality TV include the willingness to represent yourself. The UK Channel Four series *Faking It* provides a memorable illustration of this point. In this programme participants have a specific period of time to learn to 'pass' as something they are not; after this they go before a panel of judges aiming to convince. Examples of programmes analysed include a classical violinist passing as a club DJ and a factory worker from the north of England passing as a London fashion designer. The entertainment lies, we suggested, in the gruelling journey to pass and in the likely failure. Mick, the young factory worker from the north of England is tired and emotional as he speaks to camera, and in a confiding tone, about how this fashion design lark is just 'not him':

> I mean, yeah, maybe I don't not know what I like but I f*** know what I hate and this is what I hate
>
> (and he indicates the hot pink T-shirt and new hair style that are part of his 'transformation').[9]
>
> (*Faking It*, Channel Four)

The moment when this participant made a proclamation about his identity was one when our audience was prompted to care about this young man's anguish and to enjoy and laugh with or at his outspoken insistence on his identity and associated taste. This argument was developed to suggest that it is working-class participants who are called on to represent themselves and that the entertainment lies in those participants displaying that they do not have the cultural resources to know how to transform the self in the terms required for 'success' in this setting (see Skeggs, 2009). This self-representation moment from *Faking It* exemplifies the particular way in which self-representation is commonly used within reality TV programming.

Almost twenty years ago Livingstone and Lunt (1994) emphasised the positioning of ordinary people as authentic and emotional and recent work by Carpentier and Hannot repeat these findings:

> Through this relational positioning, ordinary people become articulated in Jan Publiek as authentic, but also as unorganized, apolitical, powerless, unknown, spontaneous and unknowledgeable.
>
> (Carpentier and Hannot, 2009, p. 597)

Beverly Skeggs goes further, arguing that the appearance of the audience in reality TV programmes exploits the structural disadvantages already lived by working-class people. And, in this view, the idea of 'ordinary people' in reality TV functions, more than anything else, as a euphemism for working class (Skeggs, 2009).

Internationally and over the last 20 years, the incremental findings are that where members of the audience appear within broadcast programming, be it talk shows or reality TV, they are necessarily positioned by institutional, textual and cultural processes of mediation (for example, the programme formats, the positions from which they are invited, or instructed, to speak and to which their representations are limited) which repeatedly emphasise the same kinds of characteristic, culminating in the impression that participating audience members are 'ordinary people' and that ordinary people are emotive, irrational, the location of experience, feeling and authenticity, working class and, very often, white.

I suggest that particular generic conventions associated with self-representation are being used in reality TV and, importantly, that they are familiar because they are routinely seen in quite different sites within digital culture. In a recent discussion of the audience's increased familiarity with the process of filming and consequent scepticism towards factual images, Ellis observes that factual images are quite distinct in different media, with the particular exception of what I am calling the genre of self-representation:

> It remains a different class of activity to make a documentary for broadcast and to make a recording for YouTube circulation. Different rules apply, and different expectations are held by viewers of the two media. The closest the two media get is in the status of social-campaigning videos on YouTube, and the status of highly first-person documentaries on TV. However in normal practice the distinction between amateur and professional intentions remains relatively clear.
>
> (2010, p. 187)

The example of the exasperated and almost tearful to-camera moment in *Faking It* (above) recalls the first-person mode of address to which I referred in discussing Dai Evans' digital story. And yet neither the ways in which these two textual self-representations came to be, nor who they can represent, nor how their respective success was measured remotely resemble one another, as becomes clear when we address cultural and institutional processes of mediation.

Capture Wales: cultural mediation

In this section I address the question of how the experience and views of the participating audiences shape the self-representations. Interviews with participants in *Capture Wales* destroy any notion that audiences participate simply or only because they want to represent themselves in the media. Instead, as well as imagining and hoping to reach different kinds of audience, reasons for participation included: being a 'joiner', that is to say, someone who often takes up opportunities to participate, whatever they may be; having an interest in writing, skills development and skills sharing, particularly related to ideas about 'new media'; wanting to construct a private record – like an updated photo album – and related personal, even therapeutic, aspects.

> **'Maria'**: Ask how people, on the workshops experience, rather than the motivation of the BBC. I think, for me, I haven't even questioned that, I've just focused on how it's impacted on me and my experience of it.
>
> Group interview with participants in *Capture Wales*

> **'Rebecca'**: Yeah it was much, much more for me. Something I wanted to do for myself, yeah. I mean I didn't even think about it being on the website and people viewing it.
>
> Individual interview with 'Rebecca', participant, *Capture Wales*

> **'Vikram'**: But I'd sort of told the story from my Grandmother's point of view yeah.
> **Interviewer**: Mm.
> **'Vikram'**: Somebody who I'd never met, but who I then met really through that. So it was sort of beneficial, you know. I mean okay, the BBC got a little story out of it but for me it was much bigger. Much bigger, because I, I then learnt so much about her, I then got into doing our family history also.
>
> Individual interview with 'Vikram', participant, *Capture Wales*

These kinds of view on the purposes of participating emphasise appreciation of the provision of expertise to help and encourage people to look at and to use their own family photographs, and even to look at and consider their own identity and experiences. For participants who spoke about their participation in these terms, the most important function of participation was a private one. Imagining an audience was very important to some participants, but in quite a range of ways. Some ideas about ones' own 'stories' fits into a discourse about authenticity, whereby the authentic is reached through 'real', and personal, experience. Such linking of personal experience with authenticity echoes academic and public debates about the representation of 'ordinary people', as discussed in Chapter 2. Indeed some participants are well aware that the perceived authenticity of their experience helps to validate the public service intentions of the BBC and another, linked idea is that facilitating self-representation leads to a wider set of representations overall, as 'David' implies,

'David': I think it's good. I think it's good because, rather than get stories which are from the usual place, you get a story now and again coming from their ...
Interviewer: From their area?
'David': Yeah, from the viewer if you like, rather than from management.
(Individual interview with 'David', participant, *Capture Wales*)

For some, self-representation is seen as political, so that participants talked about having a voice and 'being heard', suggesting that the process of taking part in the projects afforded them valuable recognition of their point of view and experience. This view picks up on the rhetoric deployed by the institutions when they propose that these projects 'give voice' to the public. Some suggested that their participation in the projects might lead to their being heard now, in the present, not in the future, and not only for the sake of an understanding of how we lived in the past. For example, 'Vikram', a *Capture Wales* participant, said he hoped his digital story might prompt British people to reconsider their attitudes to refugees.

Many people wanted to make digital stories that were distinct from those of all the others, continually playing with ascriptions of ordinary and extraordinary in relation to themselves and other participating audiences:

'Violet': Yeah, yes, yes. We saw all the efforts that other people had made and we were told to look on the website, but I thought I'd prefer not to because I didn't want to be influenced by other people's ...

Interviewer: Mm.

'Violet': stories, I wanted to make mine as original as I could.

(Individual interview with 'Violet', participant, *Capture Wales*)

It was quite interesting, one lady was from Pakistan and she'd come here when she was 15, had an arranged marriage and she actually was more shocked at my parents' green shed, and I was so shocked at her story and she was really shocked at mine and I thought, well mine's not half as shocking as yours but [laughs] she seemed to think it was and I mean that was quite interesting, the sort of feedback you get from the other people.

(Individual interview with 'Rebecca', participant, *Capture Wales*)

'David': Yeah, yes, it is, showing an ordinary family, and showing, you know, where is he then, well he's out there with the other family, you know [laughs].

Interviewer: [laughs]

'David': You know, out of the way kind of thing [laughs].

(Individual interview with 'David', participant, *Capture Wales*)

Participants in *Capture Wales* claim their ordinariness and in so doing expand the definition of that idea; indeed this is one of the reasons self-representation is important. And yet, as discussed above, the framing and the grouping of so many self-representations by members of the public does function to construct the 'ordinary person' in a way that contains and limits what it can mean. However, as we repeatedly see, this is not a stable and unchanging definition, but one that comes undone and must be continually remade.

Powerful ideas about 'new media' inform audience members' views of technology, institutions and even human communication and development more generally. Yet while digital technology is understood to be important, its value is unclear and shifting. Some participants emphasised skills development, others focused on audiences for the self-representations who, thanks to technology, can be reached across distances of space or time; the ability to imagine a future audience rests on the (familiar) assumption that digital technology promises that these self-representations will be 'there forever', as 'Vikram' put it,

> But yes it is available for future generations. I found it quite interesting when you wander around that site you get so many different stories, and people are telling their local stories which are then made available to the whole of the Welsh nation and anyone else who wants to be interested. I mean, there's stories there about the North/South jealousy and rivalries and there's other stories of immigrants who've come and made a life over here. I think it's just a wealth of information. You know, it's a kind of local histories that have been recorded and they are there now forever, don't you think?
>
> (Individual interview with 'Vikram', participant, *Capture Wales*)

Capture Wales constructs an idea of community – individual self-representations are made in groups and emerge from the interactions between individuals. Indeed, the group interaction in the workshops is described by those involved in digital storytelling projects in general as 'community building' and is regarded as a key aspect of the digital storytelling form (Lambert, 2006) by its creators as well as by participants:

> Interviewer: So but do you, as a more general user of the BBC, do you think it's something you would hope that they would continue to do, more people would get the chance to do, or?
> 'Violet': Well it does in a way bring the community together, which is really what the BBC's about I suppose, isn't it.
> [...]
>
> (Individual interview with 'Violet', participant, *Capture Wales*)

At the same time, the self-representations are of individuals – individual members of the community, the workshop, the local or the ethnic group. In these projects individuals represent themselves and those self-representations are located in/come out of what the project producers/policy makers/cultural commentators describe as 'communities'.[10]

'Community' functions as a uniting term, as one of the participants, 'Amy', who is herself a community arts worker, put it,

> I was going, and that's the whole other thing about the project is that everybody is equal. And that's the whole thing about community actually. We're all equal, in the community we're equal.

'Amy' in a group interview with participants in a *Capture Wales* workshop, South Wales town on border with England. The women quoted here are all white and their ages range from twenties to forties.

But, as discussed in Chapter 2 and as these interviews attest, there is not *one* united community, but rather people understand themselves as members of distinct communities and, indeed, as Bauman, for example, argues, the notion of community is predicated on exclusion of some (Bauman, 2001). Further, in a similar way to what I have described as taking place with the concept of 'ordinary people', the concept of community is undone by the uniqueness of the self-representations brought together under that label. To reiterate Mayo's succinct summary of the problems raised by what she calls 'community as policy', she notes,

> 'Community as policy' also raises problems of representation and democratic accountability. … So who can legitimately speak for whom and how can the interests of the least powerful and most marginal be represented as well as the interests of the most articulate?
>
> (Mayo, 2006, p. 394)

In the sphere of cultural representation (as opposed to political representation), the facilitation of self-representation goes some way towards addressing the problem Mayo raises here of 'who can legitimately speak for whom' (ibid.). Members of the groups taking part in *Capture Wales* represent their own, individual experiences and points of view. In this view, the notion of community does not categorise and constrain them because they speak for themselves. But, at the same time, once the self-representations are produced and displayed, these individual self-representations might well be read (by a wider audience) as standing in for wider communities, whose experiences these self-representations are taken to represent. So the problem of who speaks for who in a community is not entirely resolved – indeed, probably cannot be. Indeed, interviews with *Capture Wales* participants and producers attest to the assertion that community has a range of meanings – inhabitants of a locality, members of an ethnic group and inhabitants of a nation. And, although the meaning slides between these senses, it is assumed to be both known and also knowable.

Ideas of community as local, as ethnically based, as national, work to undermine the coherence of the notion of community. In answer to the question raised in Chapter 2 as to how the concept of community shapes self-representation, the different ways in which the term is used by those involved in *Capture Wales* attest to the contradictory nature of a concept that can both categorise and constrain the people it describes, but also support and enable them. The question that seems to follow from this is whether these subtleties in meaning-making of community and ordinary people and purpose would also take place in the making of the self-representations we see in reality TV programming. I suggest that the answer here is a clear 'no'. Despite similarities in textual form, we know that the processes of production of reality TV, and other examples of broadcasting in which members of the audience represent themselves, do not allow *the space* for cultural mediation processes to operate in the way that they clearly did in the making of *Capture Wales* digital stories.

Designations of quality are at the heart of people's understandings and expectations of what they were doing in representing themselves in *Capture Wales*. Interviews reveal disruption of the received meanings and signifiers of quality – and an expanded definition overall. Thus, for some, quality lies in the pleasure of being taken seriously, for others in the refusal of the positioning constructed by these projects. Quality is associated with the capabilities of the technology and with people's abilities to master it. So, some particularly IT-literate participants in *Capture Wales* talked about the 'poor quality' of the shorts viewed through RealPlayer on the Internet and discussed the BBC website's reliance on RealPlayer as a drawback. For some participants the quality of the outcome is completely linked to the skills developed through the professional assistance provided, while for others the technology presented a barrier to repeating the opportunity of self-representation because of issues of access and use. Furthermore, it was clear that some people have no interest in using the internet and would prefer to view the stories on TV, implying that the 'quality' of the TV viewing experience was preferable. This lack of interest in using new media technologies has been found in other studies (see, for example, Selwyn, 2003).

Some participants emphasised the ways in which they felt *valued* by the trainers, by extension by the BBC and, by implication, by society – thus the formal screening at the end of each workshop was seen as signifying quality in this sense. A related understanding of quality as value appears in several of the participants' accounts. In this view, quality is not seen as residing in production values, skills training or how the outcome is displayed. Rather, quality is seen to be inherent in the *content* of the self-representation, which is understood as the property of the person making the self-representation:

> 'David': Because if you're looking for the quality story, they don't come very often. Because … they're like leaves on a tree, they're all the same, but they're all different.
> Interviewer: Mm.
> 'David': But, er, some particular leaves will stand out from the other leaves.
> (Individual interview with 'David', participant, *Capture Wales*)

In this account, the ascription of quality changes direction. That is, quality is not about the production of the self-representation and the way that the experts facilitate this in the process or in the outcome. Instead, quality is an innate aspect of the self-representation – it comes from the raw material that the individual is providing to the institution. This takes the notion proclaimed by the institutions – that there is so much of value in people's experience – and suggests that, in among all these 'ordinary' accounts, there will be some material of quality to compete with the rest of BBC content. Notable here is the way in which the generic boundaries of self-representation are completely refused.

Skeggs (2009) argues that participants in reality TV bring limited resources, they then struggle to tell the self in the mode required and consequently they represent a self that is lacking and thereby fits what she understands as the requirement of reality TV to display attempts to improve the working-class self in line with a middle-class ideal – the entertainment lies in the structural inability for these mostly working-class participants to tell the self successfully – that is, to become the middle-class self who knows how to do this self-representation mode. This is not an expanded notion of quality and particularly a valuing of experience, but quite the opposite. To address properly the question of cultural mediation in self-representations on reality TV would require researching participants and producers. Nevertheless, existing research does suggest that this extraordinary space for cultural mediation processes to take place *does not* occur in the making of reality TV – participants are simply not as involved in the making of the textual self-representation and they are not *invited* to develop the resources to which Skeggs refers above nor to positively value and represent the resources that they already do have.

Karen Lewis, then Production Manager of *Capture Wales*, commented in her interview that this was 'crucial' and was what distinguishes *Capture Wales*:

> Whatever else happens, the experience of the people in the workshop, and their relationship with us, is crucial. And once they start doubting that, and once they start feeling that they are just fodder for TV and will be treated like every other TV contributor, then I think the project is doomed, personally. Because that's what makes it special, that's what makes it different and the relationship between the team and the people in the workshops is crucial. And that's why picking the team is very important.
>
> (Interview with Karen Lewis, Production Manager, *Capture Wales*)

Certainly, the feedback from the workshop participants does suggest that the emphasis placed on the workshop pays off:

> But it's *quite* extraordinary on the feedback forms, you get this kind of, you know: how much experience have you got with computers to date? And you know, on a scale of one to five, that's often a kind of one or two, and then all the questions about the value people put on the experience are all, kind of, up at five, I mean really it's extraordinary.
>
> (Interview with Mandy Rose, Editor, New Media, BBC Wales)

I now turn to examine the processes of institutional mediation in *Capture Wales*, by which participants seem to have been valued and self-representations consequently became more expansive than those produced in some other contexts.

Capture Wales: institutional mediation

The discussion in the preceding section established that processes of production are crucial to the emancipatory meaning of self-representation – it cannot be read off textually. In this section I explore the processes of institutional mediation shaping self-representation in *Capture Wales*. I tell a story of complexity of levels and dimensions in the organisation and of this complexity converging on experiments in self-representation in digital culture and of shifting attitudes to their value.

Participants in *Capture Wales* were understood as being ordinary people. But, as soon as the term 'ordinary people' was uttered, it was qualified. For example, Gilly Adams, who was leader of the storytelling circle for *Capture Wales* and Head of the Writers' Unit, BBC Wales, in describing the project participants, said: 'ordinary people, quote unquote if there is such a thing'.[11] Adams wanted to clarify that she did not mean 'ordinary people' in a denigratory sense. Daniel Meadows, Creative Director of *Capture Wales*, was explicit about his reasons for avoidance of the term 'ordinary people', suggesting that it suggests that individuals stories are not each extraordinary. Adams and Meadows' qualification and avoidance of the term 'ordinary people' supports Highmore's observation that there is a paradox at the heart of the ordinary because the extraordinary is central to the ordinary (see discussion in Chapter 2).

At the same time as avoidance seems to be called for, the emotive power of the term 'ordinary people', in the citizenry and celebratory senses of the term, meant that it was used in the rhetoric surrounding *Capture Wales*. For example, this term was used when the projects were promoted. Indeed, in describing *Capture Wales* to an audience of professionals in the digital storytelling field, Daniel Meadows said, 'for the first time [...] members of the public, ordinary people, that is'.[12] Here, Meadows purposefully invokes the celebratory and citizenry senses of the term. Using the term 'ordinary people' means raising the question – where does power lie? In the case of the *Capture*

Wales' invitation to members of the public to represent themselves, because people are invited to participate in a project that is devised by the professionals, they must fit their story into a shape that has ultimately been decided by the professionals. At the same time, however, the *Capture Wales* team use their position and status to open up a space for people who do not have that status and do not therefore have access to equipment, skills and a platform for display. It might be that the power relation between producer and public implied in Couldry's 'ordinary worlds/media worlds', as discussed in Chapter 2, is an unavoidable aspect of projects like *Capture Wales*, which must be acknowledged, but which does not necessarily undermine all of the project aims. Important, and political, aims include improving the media literacy of members of the public, shifting the balance of who it is that has the opportunity to represent themselves and widening the existing range and types of representation that are in circulation.

A Greg Dyke era (2000–4) strategy for the BBC nations and regions was entitled 'Connecting Communities'. According to the interviewees at BBC Wales, Menna Richards, then Controller of BBC Wales, saw the potential to fulfil this goal in the *Capture Wales* project. For example, Mandy Rose, then Editor, New Media, BBC Wales, said in interview,

> Menna saw that money as really important for BBC Wales to get out there, become more connected with the community and, as part of her connecting community strategy, she allocated a substantial portion of the money that Wales got, to New Media and, in particular, to some projects within New Media that were about getting much more local; getting into a much more direct relationship with the public and facilitating the public in having a voice on BBC platforms.
>
> (Interview with Mandy Rose, Editor, New Media, BBC Wales)

The decision to give the green light to funding *Capture Wales* suggests that management regarded *Capture Wales* as an opportunity for the BBC to fulfil its public service remit. In the wording of the Connecting Communities strategy, this public service agenda is described in terms of 'community'. The public are here being described as the community in precisely the period that Mayo has suggested saw 'community as policy' (Mayo, 2006).

Capture Wales is described in the original proposal for its funding as *Welsh Lives* and was linked to the BBC Connecting Communities strategy, which referred to plural communities. Thus the concept of community here operates at the national level, but also at the local level – where people live. At the same time, 'community' was used to describe ethnic or language groups – the Welsh language community, the English language community and ethnic communities living in Cardiff. Finally, 'community' is understood as being problematically *absent*, so that *Capture Wales* was regarded by members of the production team as a project which was about 'community building'[13] and the intention was that community would be built across groups, across difference. Thus, the aim was to include a diverse group of participants in each workshop. Simultaneously, the *Capture Wales* participants were understood as actually being 'the community', so that working with '*communities*' is understood as self-explanatory; this use of the term 'community' is ubiquitous in internal documents, such as the original funding proposal:

> An original and sustainable contribution to community self-expression. A new way for the BBC in Wales to connect with communities, not in a top-down corporate manner but through a project which depends for its delivery and success upon action within communities
>
> (Internal BBC document *Welsh Lives*, original *Capture Wales* proposal)

If it is first qualified, 'the community' can have wider usage, as in the phrase 'the business community', but, on its own, 'the community' refers to the working-class/poor/ethnic-minority residents of Wales. Thus, 'community' is naturally there – it is the site where the 'ordinary people' can be located – and, at the same time, the lack of community is perceived to be a social problem that the institution hoped to redress through workshops which aimed to bring about this amorphous thing, community.

It might be that the textual displays of diverse members of the public, brought together as a community in the *Capture Wales* project, represent a continuation of the ethos articulated by Rose when she was producer of the original *Video Nation*:

> You have to contend with and find ways of working with, and across, what may feel like, kind of fissures or fractures or deep divides, at worst, within a society. And actually *Video Nation can* perform an important function within that, which is just to kind of keep in mind that those people who you may see but never actually encounter in a day to day way as people, you know, that whoever they are, whether it's (it's not just about race, but I think race and cultural difference is a very important aspect of it) but that you keep on being reminded that actually they share a lot of things in life, about life, about humanity, *with you.*
>
> (Interview with Mandy Rose, July 1999)

In this view, the role of public service institutions in providing a forum for members of the public to represent themselves to each other is a political one. 'Community', here, as articulated by Rose, is a more politically conceived version of 'community' than that articulated in the BBC's Connecting Communities policy (BBC, 2003). Rose's argument foregrounds the serious challenges in terms of communication between groups in a differentiated society. The Connecting Communities policy was arguably different, being about the BBC connecting with its audiences, defined as a range of communities. Thus there is a tension between the building of community across difference which we see happening in projects like *Video Nation* and *Capture Wales* and the connecting with different communities that is articulated as a management goal – and this is a goal that might yet be approached differently, as we see in the 2011 BBC online strategy, below.

As we have seen, the workshops and production process of *Capture Wales* were of the utmost importance to the project team. And, at the same time, the participants are members of the audience and it was vital that they had a positive experience of working with the institution. Outcome was important because the self-representations were produced by the BBC and must meet both the standards of the institution and the expectations of its audience for a certain quality of text, as Mandy Rose noted,

The license fee essentially is about content, so we felt it was really important that the workshops produced the kind of content that we could publish.

(Interview with Mandy Rose, Editor, New Media, BBC Wales)

'The kind of content we could publish' suggests high quality content. Others involved in the production of *Capture Wales* also emphasise the high quality of the finished texts as part of what was distinctive about the *Capture Wales*.[14] Maggie Russell's comments on this subject show how the BBC viewed the *Capture Wales* digital stories:

You know, we have delivered the very best to the people who've made them in terms of our editorial experience, our teaching experience and our technical experience. That matters, the benchmark is high. People don't make crap digital stories when they work with us, but they still feel they're their stories.

(Interview with Maggie Russell, Head of Talent, BBC Wales)

But, as is also discussed in the context of museum and art worlds (Chapter 5), the idea of a quality outcome is complicated because the self-representation is always framed as a *self-representation by* a member of the public, ensuring that even the 'high quality' self-representation will never be judged alongside professionally produced content that is not self-representation. In this way, self-representation remains in a category of its own.

Daniel Meadows regarded the *Capture Wales* project as explicitly political. The aim was to train people in a visual and verbal storytelling language, so that they had the opportunity to represent themselves well in the form that they were learning and thereby communicate successfully rather than only being communicated *to*. In this way, the aim of *Capture Wales* was to deliver quality of process *and* quality of outcome – and, from this perspective, these are inseparable because the idea is that a high quality process involving highly skilled practitioners running the writing workshops and the production workshops, coupled with the use of the highest end professional-standard computers and programmes, will inevitably produce high quality outcomes.

The data suggests that there is tension between the two goals of quality of process and quality of outcome, even when the aim is to deliver both. The requirement for quality of process means that the outcome must be risked because the process is an open one, and even that the institutional brand must be resisted to some extent. The requirement for quality of outcome must mean that the process cannot be left entirely to run its own course and lead where it may because there is some emphasis on completing a text that bears some of the professionalism of the host institution. Different criteria for judging quality are deployed depending whether the focus is on quality of process or quality of outcome.

Capture Wales is rooted in community arts practice, where the focus is on process and in which the process is open to being shaped by the participants in each workshop. As Joe Lambert, one of the founders of the Digital Storytelling Center in Berkeley, California put it in a speech to the Digital Storytelling Conference in Cardiff in 2003: 'we shouldn't know what we're doing.'[15] However practitioners of digital storytelling within the BBC must produce a publishable outcome, as Meadows noted,

> But you know, the trick was to try and take this sort of art therapy practice and use it as a tool for people to be able to make their own television.
> (Interview with Daniel Meadows, Creative Director, *Capture Wales*)

But it was equally important to those working on *Capture Wales* to focus on the quality of the processes of production – the workshop – and, in particular, members of the team emphasised that their relationship with participants was unique within the wider context of broadcasters' representations of ordinary people.

Maggie Russell, then Head of Talent, BBC Wales, spoke specifically about the quality of the people running the workshops – the *Capture Wales* team:

> **Maggie Russell:** Now what is fantastic is, I haven't heard one story in four years of somebody having a bad experience making a digital story.
> **Interviewer:** Yeah, I find that bizarre [laughs].
> **Maggie Russell:** Which is, well I think it's to do with the quality of the team that are delivering it.

Interviewer: Yeah.
Maggie Russell: It's not bizarre, it's to do with, we are probably one of the highest quality community media teams anywhere in the UK.

(Interview with Maggie Russell, Head of Talent, BBC Wales)

Quality was also repeatedly invoked in reference to the technological hardware and software used by the projects. Thus Meadows and other members of the team spoke in their interviews of the relative benefits of different kinds of computer and different packages for the display of the digital stories, in terms of their quality.

According to Meadows, this digital storytelling project was unique in broadcasting because it gave 'the people access to the tools'. Let us look at what this actually entailed. Each month the *Capture Wales* team ran a five-day workshop (in English or Welsh) for ten people in towns and villages across Wales. The workshop team most often consisted of the creative director, the script consultant, two researchers and two workshop trainers, though the make-up of the team differed in the Welsh language workshops in order to ensure that the majority was Welsh-speaking. Two weeks prior to the start of the workshop selected team members ran a presentation evening in the workshop location to elicit applications. Two weeks after the presentation evening a 'gathering' took place at which the ten successful applicants met, watched digital stories and asked questions. There were also usually icebreaker and storytelling games at this stage and participants began work on their stories. One week after the gathering was a day of storytelling games and activities, which ended with each participant having finalised the text for their digital story. The second day of the workshop was for 'image capture' wherein members of the BBC team assisted in the preparation of digital images. During the next week people worked on their stories at home and the BBC team considered the scripts. A week later the three-day production workshop took place, where people learnt the computer packages Adobe Photoshop and Premier, and completed their digital stories. The three-day workshop culminated in a screening of all the stories made in that workshop. By the end of the project in 2008 'nearly 600 stories were produced' (Meadows, 2011).

Completed digital stories were uploaded to the *Capture Wales* website where they were searchable by the following themes:

challenge, community, family, memory and passion. The stories were also searchable by area, for which the web user clicked on locations on a map of Wales. In addition there was a slot entitled, 'this week's story' in which a story was promoted and contextual information offered. There was also space for the web user to respond to the story.[16] A selection of digital stories was shown on TV: on BBCi, on BBC One Wales' main evening news and current events programme, *Wales Today*, and on the Welsh language channel S4C. In addition, the audio tracks from selected digital stories were played on BBC Radio Wales and Radio Cymru.

The original proposal for the *Capture Wales* project summarised the aim thus: 'To create a project which uses digital, multi-media story telling in Wales as a way of connecting the BBC more closely to communities'. The proposal continues:

> This is a type of work which has its roots in community arts and oral history, which stretches from pre-literacy cultural traditions to recent phenomena, like BBC 2's Video Diaries series. There is also a precedent for a broadcaster-led initiative of this kind in Canada (www.storyengine.ca).
>
> (Internal BBC document *Welsh Lives*,
> original *Capture Wales* proposal)

In addition, one of the project aims was to encourage sustainability whereby partner organisations, 'in the community', could apply for public funding and set up digital storytelling projects of their own, on which the BBC team would act as advisors. It is clear that this project for sustainability continues to work well; there are a number of digital storytelling projects running in Wales and globally that follow the Californian and the Welsh examples (Center for Digital Storytelling, 2011; Meadows, 2011).

Capture Wales was part of a trio of projects run by the New Media department. The three projects came under the umbrella of *Digination* and consisted of *Capture Wales*, *Community Studios* and *Where I Live* sites.[17] These projects all contributed to the BBC Wales' Connecting Communities initiative. The BBC Wales Annual Review 2002–2003 stated,

> At the heart of these projects is a desire to establish a dialogue with communities through the sharing of skills and stories, the

discovery and nurturing of talent, and the exploration of both our heritage and our future potential. Such a dialogue will influence the way we work in the future, enrich our output and enable communities to become more actively involved in the broadcasting process.

(BBC Wales Annual Review 2002–2003, 2003)

Capture Wales set out to give members of the public living in Wales a voice on a BBC platform – in other words, to facilitate self-representation. In addition, *Capture Wales* aimed to contribute to 'Wales' New Economy', 'the knowledge economy', by providing skills in new media usage. The original project proposal promised: '[A] boost to the Welsh creative economy – which is a crucial aspect of the development of the so-called "new economy" in Wales' (Hargreaves, 2001). Finally, *Capture Wales* sought to contribute to the core BBC role of providing content for consumption by audiences.

We can understand *Capture Wales* in a context of attempts by the BBC to provide opportunities for audience participation and to provide its audience with training in the skills required to engage with new media. For instance, in the Open Centre initiative, BBC community centres delivered media literacy skills training and encouraged people to take part in the production of content for things like *Video Nation, Where I Live* or shorter versions of digital storytelling, *Shoe Box Stories*. The production of content is one of the ways in which public participation is encouraged by the institution; thus in 2004 the BBC had around 40 'user generated projects', according to Carole Gilligan, then Editor of *Video Nation*, who observed,

> but also the importance of user generated content is growing in the BBC. It's actually, we've come full circle in that it's suddenly got a really huge place because [...] there's a feeling that we actually don't connect with our audience. The fact that there are people out there that have just got great stories to tell.
>
> (Interview with Carole Gilligan, Editor, *Video Nation* Online)

The way in which the development of user-generated content is primarily framed here in terms of 'connecting' with the audience is analogous with the encouragement of participation in the museum and heritage sector to which I turn in Chapter 5. Thus it would seem that in both museums and public service broadcasting self-representation was embraced as part of the enthusiasm for user-generated content which, in turn, is embraced as a form of participation, and the opportunity for participation is seen to be one of the ways to justify public funding in the contemporary context. And typical of this discourse are words like 'participation', 'engagement', 'connection'. But representation was also important.

For the creative director of *Capture Wales* and many on the team improving the range and type of representation in broadcast spaces was precisely the political project of digital storytelling on a BBC platform. Meadows argued that enabling self-representation within the BBC, and in broadcasting more generally, constituted a significant contribution to the health of the democracy:

> No one has ever given people the tools of production; they've only eked them out, little by little. Oh yes, well you can take a Handicam and film yourself, you know, crying over the loss of your boyfriend but we're going to edit it. You know, that's gone now and it's fantastic, you know. And that we've managed to achieve that is for me, that's where the ground's been broken, that's the difference we've made.
>
> (Interview with Daniel Meadows, Creative Director, *Capture Wales*)

Self-representation has the potential to support a more radical political view than other forms of participation precisely because the aim is to allow people to represent themselves, rather than to be represented by others. Huw Davies, one of the trainers on the *Capture Wales* workshops, articulated another point that was often made in interviews by the producers involved in the day-to-day running of *Capture Wales*. In this view, the digital stories provided a welcome opportunity to *lessen* mediation and, at the same time, to challenge the usual way in which the media represent people, as Davies puts it,

> And it's punk because it's allowing 'ordinary people', in inverted commas, to make television, and just make a document, a record of the time. This is another lovely upshot of this: Wales is stereotypically coal resin miners, rugby players, stuffed sheep, daffodils, all that kind of thing, male voice choirs. We've got 260 odd films

and most of them things are either not being represented or have only been represented once. We're not stereotypical.

(Interview with Huw Davies, Trainer, *Capture Wales*)

Addressing problems in representation is not a straightforward matter. Efforts to broaden the range and type of representations in broadcast spaces have also meant an emphasis on the problematic idea we have already encountered (above) that 'ordinary people' are authentic and that this authenticity is visible only via the representation of first-person experiential narrative – in other words, ordinary people can only speak from experience. Thus, at the International Digital Storytelling Conference at BBC Wales in 2003, Pat Loughrey, Director of BBC Nations and Regions, said: 'sometimes you get the sense in the BBC that authentic, real voices, need to be interpreted to be communicated'. Loughrey went on to locate *Capture Wales* in a history of the BBC. He suggested that Lord Reith's BBC was a paternalistic institution, which understood its role as educating the audience by giving it access to great ideas. Loughrey then suggested that another key aspect of the BBC has been that of the voyeur, suggesting that often at the BBC 'real lives' are observed, told and shaped by BBC professionals. He claimed that digital stories reverse this trend and are therefore rightly understood as 'revolutionary'. Loughrey also spoke of the 'validity', 'truth' and 'extraordinary emotional power' of the stories produced by *Capture Wales*.[18] Loughrey's view of *Capture Wales* is that it provides the audience with access to the real and that this is a more authentic reality than that delivered by documentary, because people are making their own representations. A similar view was evident when Dai Evans, a *Capture Wales* participant, was given a standing ovation when he stormed the stage at the International Digital Storytelling Conference in Cardiff in 2003. The standing ovation, and the talk of a breath of fresh air at the BBC, attests to the consensus that *Capture Wales* delivered unmediated, real people to the BBC audience.[19] Attempts to give voice to 'ordinary people' are faced with the problems that result from privileging experience over other possibilities for self-representation.

Pat Loughrey's speech, and the way in which Evans was greeted at the Digital Storytelling Conference, are two instances that highlight the ongoing debate about the purpose, and indeed relevance, of the BBC and public service institutions in the cultural sphere in the twenty-first century. In claiming that these are exactly the kinds of project in which the BBC should now be engaged, and in locating them in a particular historical account of the BBC, Loughrey effectively supports the view that public service institutions should provide a forum for the public to communicate with each other themselves.

Enthusiasm at the highest levels of the organisation was also clear. *Digital Storytelling* was highlighted in one of the many reviews carried out by the BBC leading up to charter renewal, as an example of precisely the kind of project in which the BBC should be engaged:

> 'Telling a story' is something that millions of people enjoy doing. The BBC has launched a range of initiatives that have shown that many people want to cast off their role as a passive audience and broadcast for themselves. From *Voices* through *Video Nation* to *Digital Storytelling* and *Telling Lives*, hundreds of people with no previous broadcasting experience have taken the opportunity to tell their stories. For some, it has given them the skills and confidence to change their lives.
>
> (*Building Public Value: Renewing the BBC for a digital world*, BBC, June 2004, p. 72)

However, the marginal status of these projects within their respective institutions suggests that there is no consensus on this view of the role of public service institutions. For example, there were no measures of website hits for *Capture Wales* because it is simply too small for the Audience Research Department at the BBC to take an interest.[20] The fact that these projects are seen by those involved in marketing as challenging to market suggests that they do not fit the regular view of what these institutions do and, by implication, should be doing. David Cartwright, Head of Press and Publicity at BBC Wales, spoke in interview about this marketing challenge:

> The BBC Wales' press office is set up to promote its television programmes and radio programmes. We're rather good at that on the whole. But we're set up almost to talk to the people who put together television supplements in papers in Wales, about our programmes. When you're trying to get across to them.. a rather more wide ranging concept about something, and what we're really trying to get is people to get personally involved in the BBC and to

use the BBC to get their own personal messages across really, then
we have press officers, who are not used to doing that, speaking to
journalists who have never come across this before.

> (Interview with David Cartwright, Head of Press and
> Publicity, BBC Wales)

Cartwright also suggested that the name *Capture Wales* does not
successfully communicate what exactly the project is and is therefore a lost opportunity in terms of the potential to reach wider
audiences.[21] Illustrating this point is the fact that the BBC's own
internal research into its user-generated content and community
projects found that the wider public, beyond those who participate,
do not know about these projects at all and local press coverage
attests to this fact.[22]

Initiatives involving participation and self-representation have
long been taking place in the margins of broadcasting institutions,
but their place is not at all secure. In January 2011, as the result
of a review entitled 'Putting Quality First', the BBC announced its
decision to radically 'reshape' the online part of the organisation –
BBC Online (BBC, 2011). This 're-shaping' will include dramatic cuts
across the BBC websites, job losses, the closure of most of the BBC's
social and participatory ventures, and integrating BBC sites with
social media that audiences are already using. Ian Hunter elaborated
the strategy on the BBC Internet Blog, in terms of three aims: ' "to
enrich our content"; "to bring more people to our content"; "to better
engage audiences" '. He suggested that the integration of BBC content
with external websites will enable a more social and an improved BBC
website:

> The next phase of our approach to social will be to move from a
> site which offers a few fairly circumscribed social experiences to
> one which is more social everywhere
>
> (Hunter, 2011)

It is clear that the decisions are a response to massive cuts in the BBC
budget and the consequent need to prioritise:

> Central to the new strategy is a tighter focus on the BBC's edi-
> torial priorities to make the service better, and a 25% reduction

in BBC Online's budget. Both will affect our approach to social media.

(ibid.)

Nevertheless a very specific attitude to the audience seems to lie behind the particular response to a cut in the BBC's overall budget. Firstly, it is assumed that the BBC audience already consists mostly of social media users and, secondly, that the BBC's function no longer includes the facilitation of skills development for participation in media spaces for those who are not already savvy users of social media. Moreover, the encouragement of self-representation, in order to address the limitations of professional representation of the audience by the professionals, is no longer seen as the BBC's responsibility. Thus BBC investment in projects like the, now longstanding, *Video Nation* project and, more recently, *Capture Wales* is coming to an end. And yet research continues to suggest the value of self-representation that is facilitated by the public service broadcaster. For example, in a large-scale study of user-generated content at the BBC, Wardle and Williams (2008) single out the value of digital storytelling in particular and co-production with audiences in general.

In addition to being understood as a form of participation, *Capture Wales* and other ventures like it was also seen as a process for improving the range and type of representation that appeared on the platforms of broadcast institutions, which now include websites. This recent change of direction is thus very significant: the funding of projects which seek to address a paucity in representation seem particularly vital given the broader context in which mainstream representation continues to be criticised; see, for example, the arguments about the particularly limited representation of working-class white people in UK reality TV discussed above.

Capture Wales has provided innovative forms of participation – and the facilitation of participation appears to signal legitimacy to publicly funded cultural institutions in the contemporary period. But the new policy for BBC Online aims to achieve this participatory legitimacy by integrating audiences' existing social media use beyond the BBC websites. For some in the institution, finding new ways to facilitate participation is today a proper part of innovating. So, for Maggie Russell, *Capture Wales* showcased the BBC strength in innovation whether or not it were to continue:

I mean the important thing for me is that we've done it; we've done it really well. It continues to be valid. As long as it continues to be valid, we'll continue to do it. But, you know, it may be that this has sparked off a new idea and we should be doing the new idea.

(Interview with Maggie Russell, Head of Talent, BBC Wales)

Rather than an investment in organisational innovation, the *Capture Wales* project team were invested in the digital storytelling form itself with its particular grassroots history. In both *Capture Wales* and *London's Voices* the production interviews delivered a sense of continuing the project against a background of institutional constraints.

Diverging views of and investment in the value of *Capture Wales* within the BBC institution make it unsurprising that the project came to an end; having been an innovative and exciting endeavour, it does not fit with the new directions for participation. Changing policies on participation in general and self-representation in particular suggest ambivalence within the institutions about the very value of self-representation by members of the public. This ambivalence may result from the fact that there is no clear understanding in the institutions, beyond the project teams, of what exactly self-representation by members of the public is for. The debates that have continued since the birth of public service broadcasting (discussed in Chapter 2) thus continue in the digital age. There continues to be what Daniel Meadows, Creative Director of *Capture Wales*, described as 'a gap between rhetoric and practice'.[23] It is out of a conflict over whether or not self-representation matters, that the self-representations in *Capture Wales* were produced.

Conclusion: self-representation and broadcasters

Despite the contradictions and tensions surrounding the processes of mediation shaping the self-representation that results from a project like *Capture Wales*, we must remember the broader broadcasting context in which this marginal (and now closed) project took place, that is, a production context in which, to repeat Karen Lewis' words, the participating audience can often be 'fodder for TV'. This is a context of institutional mediation in which self-representation appears across programming like reality TV, functioning as a generic mode (textual mediation) that works to engage the audience – ultimately in order to produce a profit for commercial broadcasters and high viewing figures for public service broadcasters competing in a commercial environment. Perhaps the tensions arising in the mediation-shaping self-representation in *Capture Wales* should therefore be seen, in this broader context, as productive ones – hence repeated calls for a continuing space for projects *like this*, even as we work to encourage modes of participation that move beyond restricting the participating audience to representing the self (cultural mediation) in terms of individual experience. Noting the origins of the term 'broadcasting' itself, Gripsrud observes: 'It clearly reflects a centre-periphery structure. It originally meant sowing by hand, in the widest possible (half) circles' (Gripsrud, 2010, p. 7). Referring to Durham Peters' (1999) earlier *Speaking into the Air* and Scannell's (2000) work on the democratic nature of broadcasting, Gripsrud reminds us that broadcasting in its very structure of address allowed a democracy (of listening) particularly when those structures operate within a public service remit. Referring to an article by Andrea Gourd (published in German) Gripsrud writes,

> The radically diversified digital media system might be one where specific groups' chances for self-presentation increase – while the chances that other groups are presented to them are reduced. (Gourd, 2002, p. 251)
>
> (Gripsrud 2010b, p. 13)

This cautionary note, echoing Silverstone's earlier emphasis on the question of who is listening (Silverstone, 2007), reminds us of the importance of the audience *for* the ubiquitous self-representation with which we are concerned. We know from OFCOM figures that broadcast TV continues to reach very large audiences, rendering the problem of mediated self-representation even more complex than indicated in the discussion so far. While self-representations in reality TV or other broadcast spaces reach a far wider audience than do digital stories, if the representations are limited and constrained in particular and repeated ways, then we have to say that self-representation is, mostly, not being used to democratic ends at all. Hence the heightened importance of self-representation produced under the auspices of projects like *Capture Wales* – even with the tensions surrounding the mediation that we have explored in this chapter. This means that when the cutting of projects facilitating self-representation is a response to fiscal stringency, we should be concerned about the adequacy of remaining representations of the public, in all its diversity, in the spaces provided by broadcasting institutions.

5
Museums and Art Worlds

Introduction

> People should come here and feel like it's about them
>
> Sarah Gudgin, Assistant Curator of Oral History,
> Museum of London

While any claim about trends at an international level must come with a heavy qualification that local practice differs, as ethnographic work shows best (e.g. Coleman, 2010), nevertheless museum scholars suggest a changing role for the museum's public and consequently for the institution itself. The change is summed up in the idea that museum visitors should 'tell their own story'. In this chapter, I ask what self-representation in museums is made of, what work it is doing and what tensions of mediation process it is constituted from. In Chapter 2 I suggested that there is an international discussion in the field of museum studies about the status of the museum institution and, at the same time, there appears to be a repeated construction of a self-representing public of museum visitors in spaces in which representations *by* elites previously dominated. The analysis presented points to a convergence across cultural sites (of broadcasting and museum and art worlds) onto what is now, arguably, a recognisable generic form. And yet attending to the processes of mediation delivers a picture of complexity as to the meaning, purpose and role of self-representation in this particular (and varied) part of contemporary digital culture.

The cultural studies scholar Michelle Henning draws on the work of philosopher Hilde Hein (2000) in observing what she regards as a politically problematic turn away from the display of objects and towards emphasising (and influencing) the *experience* of museum-goers (Henning, 2006). The emphasis in the emotional experience of the museum-goer (the audience) is accompanied by an investment in the development of participatory activities. In this regard museums and arts converge with broadcasters on the facilitation of self-representation. This convergence sometimes entails joint projects; for example, in the UK the BBC and the British Museum collaborated on the *A History of the World in 100 Objects* project throughout 2010. In this venture members of the public/audience were invited to contribute their own objects in order to link a personal history to recognised major historical events. Indeed it may be the case that we see more of such partnerships across cultural institutions of broadcasting and museums; the *History of the World* project was signalled out for mention on the BBC Internet Blog as being precisely the kind of integrated social media project in which the BBC would continue to be involved following the shake-up and reduction of its social websites which I noted in Chapter 4 (Hunter, 2011).

The construction of a self-representing public of museum-goers operates at the level of policy, institutional and individual artistic and curatorial practice and, of course, has ramifications for the public/participants/ordinary people whose role in relation to the practice of arts and museum institutions and professionals has come to be configured in particular kinds of ways. In other words, self-representation in museums is mediated institutionally, textually and culturally. The material in this chapter is presented in three sections. The first section discusses *processes of institutional mediation* in museum and art worlds, where I consider funding, institutions and artistic practice via a range of case studies. In section two, I explore *processes of cultural mediation* with a particular focus on interviews with participants in one such project: *London's Voices* at the Museum of London. This is followed in the third section by a focus on the question of *processes of textual mediation* via a critical textual analysis of self-representation in the Museum of London's *London's Voices projects*. The chapter ends with an acknowledgement of the problem of ascribing value to self-representation.

Institutional mediation

Institutional purposes for participation at the Museum of London

Interviews, observations and documentary analysis gathered in the UK during 2003–4 at the cultural sector funder Heritage Lottery Fund, the Oral History Society Conference and the *London's Voices* project at the Museum of London highlight the complexity of institutional mediation at work in the shaping of self representations in the museum sector.[1] While, of course, the detail of these particular examples are local and specific (see Coleman, 2010), they do illustrate in some detail exactly those wider themes which scholars note are taking place internationally in the museum sector. Specifically this empirical material and the study of *London's Voices* at the Museum of London points to the ways in which the production of self-representation is mediated by such factors as political climates and governments, policy directives, individual outlooks and professional trends, to name but a few. In the case of *London's Voices*, these institutionally mediating factors serve to bring into being particular kinds of self-representations of members of the public as *ordinary people* in *communities* – and as we have seen, ordinary people are typically framed by institutions as those people who are the locus of experience *above all else*.

At the 2004 Oral History Society Annual Conference, *Putting Oral History on Display*, the contemporary ubiquity of accounts of personal experience by the public was taken as given.[2] The history of the oral history movement was invoked as that of a political movement, which challenged both dominant versions of history and established power structures. In this view, oral history was understood as offering members of the public the opportunity to participate in the public record by contributing their own versions of their lives, in their own time – that is, to speak for themselves. At the 2004 conference the important question facing oral historians was understood as being – is oral history still a political force? That is, now that members of the public are participating everywhere across culture by representing their own experiences, is the political necessity for the oral history movement diminished?[3]

The way that first-person accounts of the personal lives of the members of the public are used in museums, and what they are used for, has become a heated issue in the oral history field.[4] Annette Day, Curator of Oral History and Contemporary Collecting at the Museum of London, noted in interview that few full-time oral historians are employed by museums.[5] This leads to a situation, which was discussed at the 2004 Oral History Society Annual Conference, in which museum curators who have not been trained in oral history are interviewing members of the public and using extracts from these interviews in museum displays.[6]

There is a view that decontextualised sound bites by members of the public used to illustrate an exhibition goes against the ethos of oral history because it takes power and agency away from the interviewee. This view was evident in some of the debate at the Oral History Society Annual Conference and Frazer Swift, Deputy Head of Access and Learning at the Museum of London and Project Manager of *London's Voices*, was one of several interviewees who raised this issue. Swift said that he understands the point of view of very strictly adhering to long-established practices of collecting and displaying oral history but, at the same time, noted that widening participation strategies benefit from inviting people to tell their stories and speak for themselves in a range of ways, not limited to traditional oral history methods.[7] The ubiquity of representations of members of the public's lives are seen by some museum staff as positive since, they argue, such accounts are now legitimate rather than marginal parts of the historical account, even where they are not excerpts from traditional full-length oral history interviews.

Clearly, a wider public than ever before has the opportunity both to participate themselves and to listen to other people's first-person accounts. In debating these issues, the Oral History Society Conference did not reach a consensus, but rather agreed that these are now contentious issues. These issues echo, for example, longstanding debates about the democratic role of the talk show and, in particular, the argument that, as Coleman put it in 1997, talk shows showcase 'the voice of the people' in condescending and limited ways (Coleman, 1997, p. 112).

The debate about whether or not self-representation has been done properly can be seen in terms of a wider question – what constitutes self-representation? Several issues arise from the 'mainstreaming' of self-representation. Is the increased ubiquity of sound bites at the cost of the member of the public's control? Is an oral history interview a valuable form of self-representation, even though the interviewer asks questions of the interviewee? Is a self-representation compromised if museum personnel edit the accounts? These questions follow from debates about the status and use of personal stories by members of the public in museum displays and they parallel questions about members of the public giving personal accounts in other spaces, such as the broadcast platforms discussed in Chapter 4.

From the perspective of contemporary funding bodies, finding new ways to facilitate participation is a proper part of innovating. This view echoes the then Head of Talent BBC Wales, Maggie Russell, in her remarks on the importance of innovation (discussed in Chapter 4). Thus in an interview about their funding strategy in general and the funding of *London's Voices* in particular, Karen Brookfield, then Deputy Director of Policy and Research at the Heritage Lottery Fund (HLF), noted that the HLF focus at that time was on promoting innovation via participative storytelling:

> Karen Brookfield: I think we're going to go on funding a reasonable number, maybe a significant number, of projects which encourage people to tell stories, and I would like to think that we're going to fund more of them that use those stories as well.
> Interviewer: Meaning?
> Karen Brookfield: Well perhaps that people came along with creative ideas for new style exhibitions or new style presentations in a historic setting.
> (Interview with Karen Brookfield, Deputy Director of Policy and Research, HLF)

Indeed under New Labour, participation was key to the legitimacy of public institutions, as Brookfield noted,

> Karen Brookfield: To do with a new Labour agenda, to do with, I suppose, the increased recognition that quality of life in Britain is about engagement and having people involved in things as well as just having the things. We're just looking at telling that 10 years story of HLF.
> Interviewer: Mm.
> Karen Brookfield: And it is very much a shift away from designated heritage, which you are told by an expert is heritage

Interviewer: Mm.

Karen Brookfield: to something, which you can participate in, enjoy and you can decide.

Interviewer: Mm.

Karen Brookfield: And I think that's just got, it has increased since '98 so that when we came to the strategic plan for 2002, it's absolutely central, and I think there'll be no way back.

(Interview with Karen Brookfield, Deputy Director, Policy and Research, HLF)

Self-representation may turn out to be a particularly successful means of encouraging participation and the even more vague notion of 'engagement'. However, in this view, it is not the fact of self-representation that is important but rather active participation, in any form. And, as Brookfield notes, this is a matter of public accountability:

> **Karen Brookfield:** So I suppose it's a kind of coming together of some of the sector's own desires plus a very strong agenda of accountability.
>
> [...]
>
> **Karen Brookfield:** And it's perfectly true that all sorts of people buy Lottery tickets, but very many of those people would have looked at heritage and said 'that's nothing to do with me'.
>
> Interviewer: Right.
>
> **Karen Brookfield:** That's a stately home, that's a castle, nothing to do with me, whereas actually this is to do with everybody now.
>
> (Interview with Karen Brookfield, Deputy Director, Policy and Research, HLF)

The need to justify public funding for museums may be a time limited, and UK specific, consequence of New Labour's increased funding for museums and the subsequent increased interest in justification for that funding. Nevertheless, the idea of engagement through participation is not a UK, party-specific status quo, as the historical overview in Chapter 2 makes clear; rather, engagement through participation is contemporary common sense. As Frazer Swift observed, the convergence of government agendas with the achieved dominant views of the museum profession makes a powerful force for shifting priorities:

> So it's coming from the government, but it's also coming from a general movement in the museum profession as a whole. And I think museums that are not responding to that agenda are not going to be well respected within their own profession. I think, you know, museums have got to move on....
>
> (Interview with Frazer Swift, Deputy Head of Department, Access and Learning/Project Manager, *London's Voices*)

Of course, a change in governmental agendas in any particular country (such as the Conservative-Liberal Coalition government in the UK from 2010) does not mean a change in museum priorities insofar as these depend on internationally developed professional norms. At the same time changes to, and cuts in, funding will undoubtedly have an impact on what it is that museum professionals prioritise and may, therefore, result in changes in the emphasis on participation and the subsequent use of self-representation as a strategy for participation – like the very recent announcement of changes at the BBC noted in Chapter 4.

Interviews with members of the Access and Learning Department at the Museum of London in 2003–4 made clear that the invitation to participate in the project *London's Voices*[8] was motivated (from the point of view of that department) by the wish to broaden their visitor profile:

> Yeah, and that's been one of the purposes of *Voices*, to find ways of representing and involving people through their stories and their voices. And that's why we wanted to try out different ways of presenting them, so those two strands about presentation and engagement.
>
> (Interview with Frazer Swift, Deputy Head of Department, Access and Learning/Project Manager, *London's Voices*)

With *London's Voices*, the Museum of London was embracing the trend in museums to encourage participation[9] as *part* of strategies for widening diversity. Interviews with producers and observation of events showed that activities that seek to encourage audience participation were varied, including, for example, performances held at the museum and targeted at specific sectors of the audience, outreach work in London schools, the existence of exhibition steering committees that include members of the public and a whole programme of events that are laid on to accompany exhibitions at the museum.

If we move from the top level of institutional mediation to focus on those museum professionals who are working on the day-to-day production of projects facilitating self-representation, it becomes clear that self-representation is not simply a form of participation equal to any other. For instance, Sarah Gudgin, Assistant Curator of Oral History and Contemporary Collecting at the Museum of London saw *London's Voices* as a project which would broaden the range and kinds of representation of Londoners that existed within the museum:

> I mean for me whatever the other aims are, a really big aim for me is that we are working with people that aren't represented, that haven't had a voice, that haven't had a chance to tell their stories, that we haven't told their stories. And it is about inclusivity and diversity. And I feel really passionately that, you know, these things need to be addressed. That history is, in London, God! It's such a multicultural place, we should be telling these stories. That people should come here and feel like it's about them
> (Interview with Sarah Gudgin, Assistant Curator, Oral History and Contemporary Collecting, Museum of London)

Interviewees from the *London's Voices* project team suggested that initially colleagues in the wider museum did not understood what the project was for or indeed why it was taking place. Subsequently the status of the project transformed into an award-winning one, which the (then) new director was proud to promote across and outside the museum. The importance of the support of key, powerful individuals is indicated in many of the interviews and is summed up by the Curator of Oral History's remarks about the (then) new director of the museum:

> He is very committed to oral history I think, which is great for us, committed to contemporary collecting and representation of

contemporary history in the museums, and working with the community, and representing diverse communities in the museum's galleries.

(Interview with Annette Day, Curator of Oral History and Contemporary Collecting, Museum of London)

These remarks confirm that the question of how marginal or central participation and self-representation are in museums is both a subject for debate and political – with a small 'p'.

The tensions contributing to the processes of institutional mediation-shaping self-representation in museums take on a material form when museums invite the public to speak for themselves. Victoria Tremble, External Exhibitions Manager at the Museum of London, suggested that successful projects would require the marketing perspective to be intrinsic to the design of a project from its inception. The need to integrate marketing into a project that is devised as it goes along creates a tension, as Tremble recognised, because the imposition of a strong brand is not easily compatible with the idea of opening a space within the museum that ordinary people (and not curators, marketers, designers) run, *and define*, themselves.

The construct 'ordinary people' is both strategically invoked, and strategically avoided, by those involved in the production of *London's Voices*. Strategic use takes place when the celebratory, citizenry and everyday senses of the term are invoked because of the rhetorical force that these senses of the term convey. At the same time, strategic avoidance takes place because of the negative connotations invoked by the denigratory sense of the term. It is even the case that, for some, the everyday, celebratory and citizenry senses of 'ordinary people' can carry negative, exclusionary, connotations. It is a risky term to invoke, carrying as it does so many associations. These contradictions are illustrated at the Museum of London; a promotional pamphlet produced in 2001 features a quote from one of the original directors:

I think some academics make a great mistake in assuming that the ordinary working man is not interested in his own history and background. I say firmly that if within five to ten years of opening we haven't got families from Golden Lane and other parts of Islington coming in for a look, we shall have missed out.

(Tom Hume, first Director of the Museum of London, quoted in the *Evening News*, 26 October 1976 (Ross and Swain, 2001))

Meanwhile, in the same institution, a member of the team at the Museum of London commented that they would avoid 'ordinary people' in favour of more inclusive terms such as 'Londoners', 'everyone', 'you', 'we'. Such simultaneous avoidance and use of the term 'ordinary people' shows that it is fundamentally problematic.

Equally contested is the practical use of the term 'community'. On the one hand, 'community' is understood as always already present; it describes ethnic or class-based groupings of people:

The outputs planned for year 3 were developed through a very fruitful community consultation process. Ideas for year 3 were initially discussed at a meeting of the *London's Voices* steering group. This group includes people who have previously been interviewed for the collection together with people experienced in community-based work, with many of the members coming from communities targeted by the project.

(Internal *London's Voices* documents: Documents summarising outputs, years 2 and 3)

On the other hand, a lack of community is perceived to be a social problem that museum outreach projects like *London's Voices* exist precisely to redress. Thus the website for the *Lewisham Voices* project appears to show a locally based, ethnically diverse community, through the graphic combination of images from the groups who participated. Indeed, Lewisham is a typically ethnically diverse London borough. However, the interviews and workshops were carried out with already existing groups and their shared experience was brought out more by the way the website was designed and less by any actual interaction between them, although there were attempts to bring the groups together, for example, in the event at the Museum of London to launch the project. The textual display of diverse members of the public, brought together as a community, in *London's Voices* fits with the ethos articulated by Rose regarding the original *Video Nation* project (as discussed in Chapter 4). Nevertheless, just as was the case in relation to the BBC's *Capture Wales*, tensions exist between the aim to construct community ties across social and cultural divides, and the aim to involve and engage a range of community groups in museum projects.

A discourse about 'quality' runs through the interviews with the producers and highlights the differences in resources (money and time) between the Museum of London project and other contemporary examples of self-representation such as *Capture Wales*, discussed in Chapter 4. Feedback for *London's Voices* focuses on a range of quality indicators. *London's Voices* set out to experiment with new ways of collecting and displaying oral histories, and extending oral history to include other kinds of self-representation. Feedback focused on assessing the various activities via a range of 'quality indicators'.

Quality was also repeatedly invoked in reference to the technology; members of the *London's Voices* team referred to the quality of the computer programmes for collecting, which were tested through the *London's Voices* project, and the financial costs, which impacted upon choices in terms of technology.

Most strikingly, tensions were felt between quality of process and quality of outcome. Cathy Ross, Head of Later London Department, Museum of London, points to the two priorities:

> I think that they are two different sorts of things; working with the community where the process of doing it is the key thing, and the collections development where, you know, you've got to keep your eye on what the outputs are.
>
> (Interview with Cathy Ross, Head of Later London Department,
> Museum of London)

The requirement for quality of process means that the outcome must be risked because the process is an open one and even that the institutional brand must be resisted to some extent. The requirement for quality of outcome must mean that the process cannot be left entirely to run its own course and lead where it may because there is some emphasis on completing a text that bears some of the professionalism of the host institution. But, as I shall discuss in Chapter 7, the idea of a 'quality outcome' is complicated since outcomes are always framed as self-representation by member of the public and as such are not judged in relation to professional productions that do not include the public.

Therapy and democracy: institutional mediating discourses

In the US context, the Smithsonian Institute proclaims an investment in participation, self-representation and new media in its key strategic documents and on its public website. And in the UK, the Museum of London's *London's Voices* project is regarded by its national funding body (the HLF) and by its peers as an exemplary project at least in part because of its facilitation of self-representation and its use of new media (Thumim, 2007).

Analysis of the discursive constructions of participatory self-representation allows us to explore which discourse ultimately gains (provisional) dominance and then to speculate as to what is established materially regarding the museum's public, that is, what kind of public is produced by a discourse favouring the expression of individual experience and not, for example, a group-based critique of social and economic structures.

The very first paragraph of the Introduction to the Executive Summary of the Smithsonian Institute's Strategic Plan for years 2010–15[10] marries technology and participation (via self-representation) in its discursive formation of who the institute's visitors are and what it is that they will do:

> In the future, one touch of a screen is all you will need to get every bit of information on any given species. Or to visit Smithsonian objects online – see them, hear them, and watch them in motion. Visitors who come in person to experience exhibitions that amaze and inspire will be able to contribute their own memories of objects and events to enrich the permanent record.

Friendliness ('all you will need'), immediacy ('see them, hear them, and watch them in motion') and participation ('contribute their own memories of objects') are articulated together in this vision of the modern museum. Clearly self-representation via personal experiential accounts is absolutely central to how the museum understands its role in society and this self-representation is discursively entwined with new media technologies. Moreover the combination of self-representation and new media technologies is presented as *the* common-sense response to the question lately discussed in the field of museum and cultural policy as to what a museum is (see Sola quoted in Macdonald above). The Executive Summary of the Smithsonian Institution's Strategic Plan, under the subtitle, 'Broadening access' goes on to state,

New tools and technology will exponentially broaden our access worldwide. [...] We must also remain relevant to visitors who come from around the world. To accomplish this, we will use new media and social networking tools to deliver information in customized ways and bring our resources to those who cannot visit in person. Digitizing objects and making them accessible online are major Institutional priorities as is exploring next-generation technologies that speak to 'digital natives' who expect to be reached online

The keywords in this statement invoke a discourse about the promise of technology. Words which litter this statement (New tools; social networking tools; digitising; next-generation technologies; digital natives; digital age) are apparently plain descriptions, but presented as they are in this strategic plan, entwined with ideas of participation, they take on an almost magical/science-fiction quality, recalling Raymond Williams' remarks on Utopia and science fiction. Williams suggests four types of utopian fiction, the fourth being 'the technological transformation, in which a new kind of life has been made possible by a technical discovery' (Williams, 1978, p. 203). Public participation in museums is grounded in a celebratory discourse of technology and the media, which take as given that access and visibility equal democratic participation (see also Dahlberg, 2001).

The continual linking of new media technologies and participating publics in museum discourse is clear. When recently visited, the Smithsonian website provided a list of activities available as part of the exhibition, *1934: A New Deal for Artists*. In a similar way to the Museum of London's *London's Voices* web-based opportunities for virtual participation (here *'adding your images to our Flickr group'*) are among many activities in which the web surfer is invited to participate. It is clear from this list that the casting of public as participants has not replaced the role of museum as storehouse of history and expertise (most items on this list invite museum/web visitors to take up a traditional role of audience for objects selected and displayed by the expert curators). Nevertheless, the discourse of *participating with your experience* is made central – and made central, in major part, via media technologies. While in fact the invitation to contribute your photographs is the only item on this list which actually involves participation, the wording in the other items *sounds* participatory, especially when highlighted in hypertext – such as '*Read* selected reviews and news stories about the exhibition', '*Watch* our 1934 Exhibition Slide Show' or even '*Buy* the 1934 exhibition catalog'.

A list of apparent possibilities for participation that actually contains only one such opportunity begs the question as to whether this discursive move to citizen participation is led by governmental pressure, market motives or enthusiasm to use the capabilities of new media technologies to enable participation. Activities such as pressing buttons, navigating through a website of materials and shopping are presented as participatory. In this way, the hypertext technology facilitates the discourse of participatory self-representation so that the whole interaction with the museum (via the web) is constructed discursively to sound like one in which the public is actively involved – thereby constructing the image of an actively participating, self-representing public.

Central throughout is a discourse on technology as a facilitator of institutional participation practices that foregrounds three properties of the media: simplicity (friendliness), immediacy (do it now) and accessibility (participation). What results, as the analysis has shown, is an articulation between technology and self-representation through the two discourses: democratic and therapeutic.

The funding application for the HLF[11] funded Museum of London oral history project, *London's Voices* stated,

> Voices has two aims: firstly to develop access to our existing oral history collections and secondly, to further the cause of social inclusion by promoting opportunities for contribution and participation, and by redressing the under-representation of particular people in our collections and visitor profile. The two aims are inextricably linked.
>
> (O'Connell, 2001)

The discourse of participatory community is explicit here – 'to further the cause of social inclusion by promoting opportunities for contribution and participation'. However, at the same time it is suggested that, in the museum context, participatory opportunities are best delivered through strategies for improving representation.

Moreover, the use of the key phrase 'social inclusion' suggests that participation via self-representation is understood as explicitly serving governance agendas 'to further the cause of social inclusion'. Thus a policy document (which achieved funding) focuses on the governance possibilities facilitated via projects of participatory self-representation. The democratic function of self-representation is promised in the funding application and, more than this, the museum institution has a crucial role to play in governance, via the construction of museum visitors as a self-representing public, first and foremost. Thus the concluding sentence of the Executive Summary of the Smithsonian Institute's Strategic Plan for years 2010–15 reads,

> We envision the Smithsonian of 2015 as an international leader, an institution that influences the important debates of the day and engages a far greater percentage of the world. In short, the 21st century Smithsonian will be an institution that fulfills its vast potential to serve the nation and the world.

The sentence ' … an institution that influences the important debates of the day and engages a far greater percentage of the world' employs the self-representation discourse in its democratic function. The key words and phrases here are 'debates', 'engages' and 'greater percentage of the world'. In using the word 'debate', the ideal of democratic debate among a public is strongly invoked (e.g. Habermas, 1974) so that museum-goers are cast as members of a public, that is, as citizens able (and expected) to engage in processes necessary to a democratic society, such as debate on issues deemed of shared importance. Moreover the citizens of the democracy – the museum-goers – are no longer only US citizens who might physically attend the Smithsonian, but are also members of a global public – 'the world'– who are now able to join the debate and 'visit' the museum thanks to the capabilities of new media technologies. Here, new media are positioned as central to the democratic potential of self-representation and we might go further and say that new media (as part of globalisation processes) produce a duty for an institution such as the Smithsonian to 'engage a far greater percentage of the world'.

The Museum of London's *London's Voices* project aims included 'furthering the course of social inclusion' and the Smithsonian Institute (on a far grander scale) aims to 'engage a far greater percentage of the world'. The citizenry discourse of self-representation has a strong rhetorical force. This discourse of self-representation is ubiquitous in museum documents, describing what museums can do, and in funding applications containing aims and ambitions for new projects. Moreover this version of self-representation is, as we have seen, present in policy and scholarly discussion of the contemporary museum. However, we must ask – are opportunities for self-representation in the democratic sense actually provided? The citizenry discourse of self-representation does not, in fact, achieve dominance in the projects actually delivered by the museums discussed here – as we shall see.

Even in the promise contained in the policy documents, the discourse of self-representation invokes a therapeutic discourse at least as much as a democratic one. For example, the Smithsonian Institute promises to concentrate on 'four grand challenges', the fourth of which is 'Understanding the American Experience':

> America is an increasingly diverse society that shares a history, ideals, and an indomitable, innovative spirit. We will use our resources across disciplines to explore what it means to be an American and how the disparate experiences of individual groups strengthen the whole, and to share our story with people of all nations.

While the category of the nation, rather than of the self, is explicit in the discourse here, as indicated in the phrase 'share our story with people of all nations', the centrality of the individual self to the story of the nation is, I suggest, implicit. The centrality of the individual self is so central to common-sense narratives of American society – hence the phrase 'myth of American individualism' – and indeed to Western thought more generally, that it constitutes 'common knowledge' which does not even need to be made explicit here (e.g. De Tocqueville, 1863). Thus in this extract – 'Understanding the American Experience' – it is the individual who has the experience which, multiplied, constitutes 'the disparate experiences of groups', it is the individual who experiences 'what it means to be an American' and 'people of all nations' are always, necessarily, groups of individual persons.

The discourse of self-representation is invoked in this passage as the expression of experience and tied to the governance role of the museum institution: 'how the disparate experiences of individual groups strengthen the whole...'. Thus *experience* is to be expressed in the service of the familiar goal (recalling Jowell, in Chapter 2) in which the museum institution helps to construct and subsequently to govern the public in a particular way, as a self-expressing public (and not a democratic one). In this discourse ordinary experience is valued. The key phrase 'to share our story' suggests common knowledge that individual experience comes in the form of narratives of the self or (cumulatively) of the nation and these specifically experiential narratives are to be 'shared' with 'people of all nations'. Here self-representation as a sharing of experience is proposed as the preferred mode for interaction among ordinary people; democratic possibilities through dialogue between 'people' from 'all nations' are not emphasised with the result that the key phrase 'sharing a story' emphasises the therapeutic in the discourse of self-representation.

When we turn to practice, the emphasis shifts completely to a therapeutic discourse of self-representation. The use of oral history is instructive here. Oral history (as key phrase and as political and historical movement) developed internationally from the 1960s. Oral history offered a method for publicly valuing ordinary experience and changing whose stories, and which kinds of stories, formed the historical record in societies. Oral history is linked to notions of 'hidden history' and 'history from below' but, as Paul Thompson notes, it is developed in a range of directions (including therapeutic, democratising and, also, reactionary: 'oral history is not necessarily an instrument for change; it depends upon the spirit in which it is used' (Thompson, 2000, p. 3). Nevertheless oral history does seem to have entered the mainstream to an unprecedented degree, as the theme of the 2004 Oral History Society Annual Conference, *Putting Oral History on Display* attests,

Oral history has come of age in the public's consciousness: personal testimony is recognised as a valuable element of contemporary historical interpretation and an incomparable educational and artistic resource

(Oral History Society Annual Conference, 2004)

But the emphasis on the 'personal' in the above statement is important. As self-representation has proliferated, it has become synonymous with the telling of personal experience, sometimes – and this is the key area for debate – to the exclusion of what is political about the personal. The following is an excerpt from the evaluation of the *London's Voices* oral history exhibition carried out on behalf of the Museum of London:

The exhibition was successful in a number of ways:

- The vast majority of visitors (86%) said that it had made them think about the significance of their own experiences.
- Over three quarters (76%) said that it made them more aware of the value of the experiences of ordinary people.
- Over a third (38%) said that it had made them more aware of the cultural diversity of London.
- Everyone interviewed was positive about the value of oral history, with many highlighting its ability to make history more accessible by presenting it from individuals' personal perspectives.
- 98% of visitors had understood to some degree what the exhibition was aiming to achieve, with 40% referring to the diversity of London's population and over a third (36%) referring to the lives and views of ordinary Londoners.

(Museum of London *London's Voices*, Exhibition exit interviews)

In evaluating the success of the oral history exhibition, all questions asked (and, that is, the questions considered to be important), place emphasis on encouraging members of the public to think about the lives and *experience* of themselves and other *ordinary* people/Londoners. In this way ordinary experience is strongly validated – in keeping with the shift in museums towards providing forums for the expression of experience. Similar focus on the value of experience is to be found in the first sentence on the Smithsonian Institute's 'about' page on that institution's website:

> The Smithsonian American Art Museum, the nation's first collection of American art, is an unparalleled record of the American experience.[12]

Similarly a press fact sheet for the *A New Deal for Artists* exhibition (which is primarily about displaying traditional art objects) nevertheless includes a statement about *engaging* publics, both by inviting 'senior members of the public' to contribute with memories of the Great Depression and by inviting the public in general to engage with the museum's initiatives online: 'Details about an array of free public programs and online initiatives are available at americanart.si.edu.' And it goes on to state,

> Senior members of the public with memories of the Great Depression are encouraged to attend and record an oral history with Smithsonian Folkways Recordings, the nonprofit record label of the Smithsonian Institution.[13]

Ways of engaging via oral history are here presented as being about delivering experience, often through participatory self-representation; there is nothing (explicit) in this discourse of experience about how such a valuing of experience could (or should) link to democratic praxis.

In summary, across the documents and websites of both the museums (and the two particular projects *London's Voices* and *A New Deal For Artists*) we see the invocation of self-representation as democratic and the practice of self-representation as therapeutic expression. Arguably the rhetorical power of the practical opportunity depends on the promise of its being something more than therapeutic self-expression – that is, it depends on *invoking* democratic self-representation and the possibilities therein. Moreover both discourses of self-representation (democratic and therapeutic) are presented as inextricably linked to the revolutionary promise of new media technologies – recalling that now long-established discourse of the promise (and threat) of technology for democracy.[14]

Fine art and ordinary people: the University of Local Knowledge project

'Socially engaged arts practice' is one of the labels used to describe the practice of artists who focus on working with the public and/or in public spaces in various ways. Not a new part of fine art practice at all, pioneers in this field began this kind of work in the 1970s and before. And quite clearly there are overlaps with the authorial film-making and autobiographical film-making discussed by Michael Renov and by Dovey and Rose (Renov, 2004; Dovey and Rose, forthcoming). The label 'socially engaged arts practice' has been used in a range of ways[15] including to refer to fine arts practice where the artist is concerned with making art that has to do with social, political and cultural life, and to practice which aims to give voice to the experience of ordinary people, via forms of participation. Moreover such practice can be seen as having a revival or renewed interest in the contemporary period.

American artist Suzanne Lacy is known as a fine artist and sometimes as a performance artist, whose work has consistently involved large-scale projects giving voice to ordinary experience. Lacy recently worked in Bristol, UK, on a project entitled *University of Local Knowledge*.

University of Local Knowledge

From September 2009 to Spring 2010 Californian Artist Suzanne Lacy will develop the University of Local Knowledge (ULK), working with Knowle West Media Centre, the Arnolfini, local artists and the community. ULK aims to reveal the shared wisdom of a community built in a time of recession.

Uncover, share and celebrate the skills, talents and knowledges of Knowle West! We are currently exploring car boot sales, horses and travel, the exchange of knowledges and economic value.

ULK will launch with a series of 'actions' as part of the 100 Days initiative. More information coming soon![16]

This project is a partnership between Knowle West Media Centre, a community and media centre in a quite disadvantaged, largely white working-class, residential neighbourhood of Bristol, UK, and

Arnolfini, Bristol's premier contemporary art institution, which is located in the centre of the city. Arnolfini literature describes the project thus:

> a collaboration between Knowle West Media Centre and Arnolfini, focused on supporting an ongoing professional development programme for state of the art research between equal spheres of knowledge – community development, local knowledge, and contemporary art practices.[17]

This collaboration is between an unapologetically contemporary art gallery and a local community media centre. The Arnolfini remit emphasises its position as a cutting-edge contemporary art space before its role as a museum for all via the provision of educational activities:

> 'Arnolfini is one of Europe's leading centres for the contemporary arts, presenting innovative, experimental work in the visual arts, performance, dance, film, music and events, accompanied by a programme of educational activities [...] Arnolfini is a registered charity, core funded by Arts Council England and in receipt of regular funding from Bristol City Council'.[18]

Lacy is a leading international artist with a long-standing and well-respected engagement with a fine art practice involving collaboration and partnership with members of the public. Nevertheless the role of the voice of ordinary people in her work and other fine art practitioners must continue to be a debated question, as was clear in discussion between community workers and artists at the Knowle West Media Centre conference: *Demanding Conversations: Socially Engaged Arts Practice in a changing political climate* (September 2010). Moreover the recent governmental focus on the instrumental roles for art and culture in a democratic society further complicates the reception of the practice of artists working in this area since quite clearly funding opportunities in recent years have been linked with the participation of ordinary people in fine art projects. When this has been the case, the question arises even more as to the role of the voice of ordinary people in artists' work. An invitation to participate in a workshop for

the *University of Local Knowledge* project is found on a local community website whose strapline reads: 'We Are Knowle West: Real News
from a Real Community'.

> University of Local Knowledge ULK aims to bring together the
> knowledge and skills that exist in our area and share them with
> other people. Over the next few months we want to work together,
> transforming Knowle West's knowledge into stories and short
> films. Come to a ULK wiki workshop where you can write words,
> collect images and upload files. People will be on hand to assist
> you adding your local wisdom.[19]

Put simply, the question is – who is speaking in a project that invites
'ordinary people' to 'write words', 'collect images' and 'upload files',
but a project that is an artwork by Suzanne Lacy at the same time
as it is a community project? The answer is not straightforward and
the question is interrogated by those partners involved in this project
as part of what they do (see Knowle West Media Centre Conference:
*Demanding Conversations: Socially Engaged Arts Practice in a Changing
Political Climate* (September 2010)). This example serves to show both
the presence of self-representation by ordinary people in projects by
fine art institutions and artists and to highlight the complexity of the
mediation processes entailed. Mediation processes are struggles, even
if we only attend to the dimension of institutional mediation where
'institution' includes such diverse organisations as the Arnolfini and
Knowle West Media Centre, and professional stakeholders include
local community workers, gallerists and internationally acclaimed
artists. The dimensions of textuality and culture, as we shall see, are
similarly characterised by complex mediation processes.

Cultural mediation

When we move from the dimension of institutional processes of
mediation to that of museum visitors' own experience of participation, does self-representation appear to go beyond self-expression
(therapeutic view) and impact at the level of democratic voicing of
'difference'? Participants in *London's Voices* projects talked in interview about 'having a voice' and 'being heard', suggesting that taking
part afforded them valuable recognition of their point of view and

experience. These key phrases invoke the democratic discourse of self-representation deployed by museums, discussed above. The young people explained that they took the opportunity afforded by a photography project to show what they thought needed to change in their local area:

> 'Kimberley': No, it had to be about our local area but what we wanted to do. But we seen it as like how we wanted it to change. We like, we seen it like as we're showing the bad things what we want to change.
> Interviewer: Ok.
> 'Clifford': To improve our area.
> 'Kimberley': Yeah, to improve it. So we were showing the good things that's, like, changed and then the bad things that need to be changed.
> (Group interview with members of a North London youth group, participants the *London's Voices* project *16–19*)

In this extract, it is the democratic discourse of self-representation that is invoked because the opportunity provided by 'having a voice' is understood as self-expression for the purpose of improving the participants' everyday life (notice the multiple use of 'change' and the use of 'improve'). But, of course, the Museum of London (or any museum) not only is *not* responsible for improving housing provision in a city, but nor does its remit include channelling public voices towards those who have the responsibility to do so. In this way, self-representation loses its democratic function – making a difference – insofar as the public voices are expressive, but are not heard by their dialogic addressees – in this case, those who might do something about their 'local area':

> young people in this area are probably sort of growing used to the fact that, you know, it is probably more in vogue now for people to go out and ask young people what they think, it's probably not yet completely in vogue to then go and act on it. But they're at least now asking the questions.
> (Interview with youth worker of a North London group, participants in the *London's Voices* project *16–19*)

Whereas some might dismiss such observations by saying that these participants had misconstrued the purpose of museum participation in the first place, in fact, this youth worker's comments throw into relief the constitutive ambivalence at the heart of the concept of self-representation and its mediation – an ambivalence between inviting people's voices for the purpose of community building (democratic function) and inviting people's voices for the purpose of self-expression (therapeutic function). The youth worker challenges this process by referring to self-representation as voice in terms of 'a vogue' and by ironically contrasting this to substantial democratic engagement ('go and act on it') as 'not yet completely in vogue'.

When talking about the exhibition of their photographs which was the culmination of their participatory project at the museum, the young people themselves explained their frustration in the following terms:

> 'Clifford': A normal TV with about five chairs for people to sit and there was about thirty people.
> 'Interviewer': And whereabouts in the museum was it, when you come in the museum?
> 'Clifford': When you come, go right, it was just there.
> 'Interviewer': That sort of entrance.
> 'Kimberley': In the corridor like no one even cared about us. They didn't even put us in properly, just in the corridor.
> 'Clifford': I thought our pictures were gonna be on the wall.
> 'Kimberley': That's what I thought... it wasn't...
>   (Group interview with members of a North London youth group, that participated in *London's Voices* project, *16–19*)

The curators never promised a formal exhibition in a main gallery of the Museum of London. However, these participants recognised that their photographs were displayed in the museum as, to borrow the BBC phrase, 'amateur content' and found this disappointing. The complaint in this extract delivers a challenge to the participants' physical and symbolic location as 'ordinary people' (Couldry, 2000a). Thus museums' invitations to self-representation as therapeutic self-expression can be met with disappointment precisely because the discourse of self-representation promises more than this, invoking the idea of democratic voice as we have seen above. Bourdieu suggested a legitimacy hierarchy in 'systems of expression' in which amateur photographs are at the bottom while 'consecrated arts such as theatre, painting, sculpture' are at the top (Bourdieu, 1990 (1965)). When institutions invite members of the public to represent themselves, processes of mediation may ensure that the participants stay in their place by producing representations that are recognisably amateur and '*ordinary*', and therefore located at the bottom end of a well-established hierarchy of legitimacy. It might be that representations of '*ordinary people*' are only legitimate if they do not challenge this positioning. Moreover ordinary citizens must produce representations of experience; the legitimacy of ordinary self-representations in established systems of expression depends on *having* and *representing* experience.

The question of legitimacy emerges, however, as a two-way street. The prevalence of the discourse of participatory self-representation in museums, explored above, suggests that contemporary museums *need* participating publics in order to establish and maintain their legitimacy *as* public institutions. At the same time, publics seek legitimacy (and with it, power in the democratic society) when they accept the invitation to represent themselves in the institutions. Here we revisit Schegloff and Billig's debate (discussed in Chapter 2). Museum practices *both* confirm a community (of museum-goers as participants through the mediated self-expression of their ordinariness) *and* gloss over the power relations between participant and institution (through their hierarchy of 'systems of expression'). Thus the question of power raised by *who* tells *which* stories (and with which this book began) is not simply resolved by the presence of those stories in spaces from which they had previously been absent.

Indeed the use of new media technologies, as well as the *idea* of interactive new media technologies, is not innocent here. The very same technological properties that facilitate spaces for self-representation may also be responsible for the tip of the balance towards the therapeutic rather than the deliberative/democratic. This is so insofar as the properties of new media technologies – namely friendliness, immediacy and accessibility – facilitate visibility and exposure but do not by themselves catalyse/enable the co-ordination of more elaborate projects of deliberation, collaboration and change.[20] Moreover these same technological properties make possible the physical manipulation of self-representation within the museum space in line with its 'hierarchy of expression' so that, as discussed above, the very tools that facilitate the presence of self-representations might also facilitate a particular kind of shaping of that presence as a therapeutic and not a democratic one. I turn now to consider processes of textual self-representation.

Textual mediation

'Mr Transitional' is the title of a poem by 'Harry', a participant in a South London Library Services African-Caribbean Reading Group, who took part in the *London's Voices* project, *16–19*. Here is a teenager representing himself and the product is displayed by the Museum of London, underlining the validity and importance of his voice. At the same time, however, this self-representation is framed by a title and web page. That this framing is considered necessary implies an assumption that self-representation must be explained as such to the audience. The explanation accompanying the self-representation serves to identify it as different from more familiar representations of members of the public on view in media or in museums. The explanation alerts the audience to the proposition that this is a particular kind of content, implying it is to be read in a particular kind of way. If self-representation is a generic form, then the museum's framing alerts the audience to the kind of genre on view – representation of personal experience by a member of the public who is neither a media nor a cultural industry professional of any kind. The poem appears as typed text on a white background, as if a typed poem has been scanned. It is written in the third person. The first line introduces the characters of the piece: 'boy', 'parents', 'lover'. This poem fits into the stereotype that working-class African-Caribbean teenagers become parents at a young age. But, at the same time, the stereotype is dispelled because the situation is shown from the boy's point of view, with his 'Heart beating like a boxer pounding a punch bag'. This is not any 'Mr Transitional'; rather, it is a particular person's experience. Nevertheless, the title 'Mr Transitional' encourages understanding the poem as yet another example (like the other poems titled 'Mr' and 'Miss' 'Transitional') of a universal experience of passing from teenage to adulthood. Thus, despite the detail of 'Harry's' particular experience, the framing encourages us to consider what teenagers have in common with each other, across their evident differences.

The particularity of the detail in 'Harry's' poem is thus in tension with the framing. There is the poem – 'Harry' uses writing to make his self-representation, but this writing is scanned and fitted into a designed website that presents the collected self-representations by young people. The opening page of the *16–19* website states,

> The Museum of London collaborated with six groups of young people to represent their lives in London today. The young people involved shared their stories and opinions and reflected their lives through photography, poetry, fashion, music and oral history. Based on their own experiences and addressing issues that are important to young people in the city today, London 16–19 highlights the talent, diversity and creativity of those who took part.[21]

This frames the self-representations, suggesting that they can be understood as a relatively homogenous group. However it seems equally true that the self-representations are distinctive precisely because they look different (and are made differently) to representations of the public that are made by professionals.

'Harry's' poem, 'Mr Transitional', is written in the third person. Are we, in this distancing from the first person, being invited to imagine that this might be fiction? Does it matter? In *London's Voices*, as in *Capture Wales*, while the notion that we are hearing the truth is central, the existence of the texts and their content makes clear that whether or not this really is the truth cannot in fact be determined. Projects that facilitate self-representation draw attention to the necessary shortcomings of any one historical account. Yet these self-representations are justified as having a place on the platforms provided by public institutions precisely because they promise the audience access to a true(r) representation of 'ordinary lives'.

Tensions pull apart the construct 'ordinary people' and pull local 'community' from the individual global self. Thus, the web page for *London's Voices* lists the sub-projects that made up the overall programme of projects. Above the title and synopsis of each of these projects, a short paragraph summarising *London's Voices* as a whole is accompanied by a graphic rectangle made of eight faces of different ages and racial origins. These images suggest that London is made up of a diverse range of people, a fact celebrated on this website, by this project. The juxtaposition of faces combined with text repeatedly referencing 'Londoners' invokes a community of Londoners:

> London's Voices explores, reflects and celebrates London's great diversity through the voices, memories and opinions of Londoners. It opens up the Museum of London's rich oral history collection.[22]

At the same time as this diverse London-wide community is invoked, the idea that the city consists of a range of separate (overlapping) communities is also suggested, both through the juxtaposition of summaries of work with different groups and, sometimes, through explicit statements. The summary for *Voices Online*, for example, reads,

> Access full oral history interviews and explore the connections that we have within our families, our communities, the city and the world.[23]

That communities exist is a given in the texts of the *London's Voices* website, specifically in this macro-text, framing the individual self-representations. But at the same time a project that encourages community awareness and community building suggests that 'community' is considered to be lost and, moreover, is something that we all want back, recalling Silverstone's observation that 'Ideas of community hover between experience and desire' (Silverstone, 1999, p. 97). On the homepage of *London's Voices*, community is presented as something that we all know. Community in London is plural; in London, it seems to suggest, we inhabit a range of communities. At the same time, the existence of the project – *London's Voices* – seeks to bring Londoners together, through emphasising their shared experience; so that there is a wider and less explicit notion of London community hovering here, nearer perhaps to 'desire' than to 'experience'. Building community appears to be an intended outcome of *London's Voices*, producing another paradox; something is being built which we all know already exists.

Questioning London was another *London's Voices* sub-project, which invited visitors to the museum to complete questionnaires described as the 'Voices Alternative Census'. Two thousand six hundred questionnaires were completed and the results presented on a website. The *Questioning London* website emphasises individual experience and perspective. However, summaries are presented as statistics in the form of statements such as: 'X number of respondents said if they could change something about London it would be the transport' and exemplary quotes such as

> We asked ... how would you label yourself?
> 'A rebellious, ponderous, socialist'
> 'They are labelling me: "illegal immigrant" '
> 'Afro-centric and eclectic'
> 'East London and common as muck'.[24]

This presentation collectivises the individual experiences of London's inhabitants. Here, those individuals are shown to each other and this creates the impression that a civic community at the level of the city does, in fact, exist. Thus, on the website, community is built by the *London's Voices* producers out of individual responses to the questionnaire. And yet the showcase of the responses equally exposes the fact that, when we look into the individual texts, the idea of the London community seems to come apart. The community presented here is clearly constructed from individual experiences that are not necessarily experienced as communal. Moreover, as Morley notes, in a discussion of some earlier efforts to facilitate self-representation:

> there is still a problem of form. By far the easiest way in which to get working-class people to articulate their experience is in the form of autobiography, which is, by its nature, an individualizing and, to that extent, decollectivizing – if not depoliticizing- form. With this in mind, the Centerprise project has carefully taken the title of the 'People's Autobiography of Hackney', but its constituent units were still accounts of individual lives.'
> (Morley, 2009, p. 496)

The Museum of London explains the *London's Voices* project at the top of the front page of the *16–19* website. The summary reads,

The Museum of London collaborated with six groups of young people to represent their lives in London today. The young people involved shared their stories and opinions and reflected their lives through photography, poetry, fashion, music and oral history. Based on their own experiences and addressing issues that are important to young people in the city today, London 16–19 highlights the talent, diversity and creativity of those who took part.[25]

Photographs taken by the participants are displayed in thumbnails that the user can click to enlarge. The overall effect of the way in which the disparate individual experiences are collected is to suggest a community of 16–19-year olds in each sub-project. In one photograph, by 'Kimberley', a young woman scowls at the camera. Her light brown hair is scraped back in a tight ponytail, she wears a red hooded top, studded belt, black jeans and her long-nailed hands are on her hips. In the background a scaffold-covered building blocks out most of the sky. Big trees add to the darkness of the image, while in the background more houses contribute to a hemmed-in atmosphere. This is a striking and yet 'ordinary' photograph, combining the girl's defiant glare with the familiar tropes of the 'inner city' background. The text above the image suggests how we should understand the group of photographs – as young people's own representation of their lives in London today – and it is in this context that the photograph seems to say: 'This is where I live, this is who I am' or 'This is where we live, this is who we are'. The portrait tells us a lot about what identity the girl in red and her photographer friend want to present. The tight pony tail and long nails suggest 'street style', a style signifying 'cool' that is adopted by white working-class young people and is drawn from black working-class style (Diawara in Skeggs, 2004). At the same time, the girl in the photograph looks (to this viewer) vulnerable; the defiant look might be sad or maybe she is restrained by an overbearing background. Above the thumbnail photographs the following text is dominant on the page: 'Growing up around ******** estate in *******, this group of young people have captured local life through photography to show what it's like to be a teenager in a tough urban community.' The framing phrase 'what it's like to be a teenager in a tough urban community' is somehow at odds with the power, humour and complexity of the images. The explanatory text tells the web user what this material is – these are self-representations about X. And yet the notion of community is strange here, in the context of the phrase 'tough urban community', because 'community' usually carries positive connotations (Bauman, 2001; Silverstone, 1999). Both knowingness and humour figure in the photographs presented in *16–19*: a photograph of a pet dog through bars; a photograph of lads posing in front of scooters and graffiti and next to bags of garbage; a photograph of an old man sitting on his bed, holding a black and white photo (of himself as a young boxer); a photograph of a high rise ('this is where we are'); a photograph of kids play-fighting; a photograph of kids against the railings of a concrete sports field. Again, in the tension between the micro-texts (the self-representations) and the macro-texts (the *London's Voices* websites on which they appear), the *London's Voices* project both builds and destabilises this notion of 'community'. What is the community that these very different photographs, selected and displayed together, present? Is it really there?

The photograph of the girl in red was selected by the young people to contribute to those displayed on the *16–19* website, but the curator chose it from that selection. These self-representations are framed by the white, clean background of the Museum of London website. There is a sharp contrast between what we see in the photographs and the look of the website on which they are displayed. This background imposes an order on the self-representations – they are branded by the museum and by the particular aesthetic of the museum platform. In *London's Voices* quality is signalled in the macro-texts of the websites and TV programmes framing the self-representations. Here, quality is about the authority of the institutions and this is indicated by a serious, 'tasteful' institutional aesthetic. But, at the same time, *London's Voices* gives space to images taken by participants who were learning skills – in photography and in writing, for example. There is a strong sense, therefore, in which quality is about enabling members of the public to learn skills in order to make their voices effective. Information about these processes through which the self-representations get made is delivered in the macro-texts on the websites, hence the processes of institutional and cultural mediation become part of how we understand the self-representations *as texts*.

There is something very discomforting about treating the individual self-representations to a critical analysis as I have done here, just as a literature critic might read and analyse a poem or a film studies scholar might critique a film. Moreover, it is precisely this unease that recalls debates about the validity of textual analysis discussed in Chapter 3. The fundamental tension that flows through the institutional, textual and cultural mediation of projects like those discussed here is this – what or who are the projects for; what are the politics shaping the mediated self-representation that is taking place in this sector? But in order to address this question, as I have been arguing throughout, we are faced with the problem that won't go away – *how* to judge the *value* of mediated self-representations:

> However, if we are to offer critiques of those representations that we deem inadequate, then it also behoves us – difficult as it may be- to make explicit what exactly it is that we would regard as a good (or at least a better) form of representation and to be clear about the grounds on which our claims rest. Evidently this will get us into deep water, in which we will not easily come to agreement, as we attempt to move beyond critique alone to the specification of the criteria for adjudicating these complex philosophical and epistemological questions.
>
> (Morley, 2009, p. 503)

I return to the problem and the necessity of distinguishing between, and evaluating, self-representations in the different places that they now routinely appear, in Chapter 7. In Chapter 6, I address the self-representations that are proliferating in online spaces not provided (or mediated) by traditional cultural institutions.

6
Self-Representation Online

Introduction

Are the particular tensions constraining self-representation finally removed in the online spaces that do not belong to long-established institutions like broadcasting or museums? It is both remarkable and genuinely new that making a self-representation no longer requires intermediaries to call, invite, edit or prescribe in any way what the text produced will turn out to be. In the online setting people do not need broadcasters to provide a platform, to invite or to edit their self-representations. People do not need museums or artists to make displays or works to provide an outlet for their voices. In this never-ending platform, epitomising the possibilities of a digital culture, it seems as if 'ordinary people' might really 'speak for themselves'.

In Chapters 5 and 6, research which explored the mediation of self-representation by broadcasters, and in the museum and art worlds, found that the *idea* of the participatory internet was repeatedly invoked in policy and everyday discourses as a kind of Holy Grail – a space that radically reduces the mediation processes shaping self-representation. Indeed the practice of self-representation is widely seen as synonymous with the spaces of Web 2.0 to the exclusion of attending to the practice of social networking:

> It is this social networking function that is most noticeably absent from most mainstream media accounts of amateur and everyday content creation [...] Amateurs are represented as indi-vidualistic, self-expressive producers who are mainly interested

in 'broadcasting themselves,' rather than engaging in textual productivity as a means to participation in social networks.
(Burgess and Green, 2009, p. 29)

In this chapter I focus on social networking. I want to argue that while social networking may be the reason for participation online, self-representation is, very often, a condition of such participation. Indeed the ways in which self-representation is both a condition of participation and an opportunity are quite entangled, and it is the purpose of this chapter to try to untangle these in order to advance our understanding of self-representation in online spaces. Of course self-representation takes place in myriad more settings online than just social networking sites and includes both amateur and professional examples of the representation of self, indeed challenging this boundary at times (Dovey and Rose, forthcoming). In this chapter my focus is on how self-representation has become an everyday part of participation online, asking what that might mean, however analysis of self-representation could usefully be extended to other kinds of example of the practice.

The contemporary online environment is replete with opportunities for participation:

... Wikipedia, MySpace, Facebook, YouTube, Google, Blogger, Rapidshare, Wordpress, Hi5, Flickr, Photobucket, Okrut, Skyrock, Twitter, YouPorn, PornHub, Youku, Okrut, Redtube, Friendster, Adultfriendfinder, Megavideo, Tagged, Tube8, Mediafire, Megaupload, Mixi, Livejournal, LinkedIn, Netlog, ThePirateBay, Orkut, XVideos, Metacafe, Digg, StudiVZ, etc...
(Fuchs, 2011, p. 288)

Indeed Fuchs' list refers only to high profile examples of Web 2.0 and we could add to it a whole range of more local opportunities including, for example, geographical local communities and interest group message boards, chat rooms and newsletters. Moreover, recent scholarship on the notion of pervasive media suggests an ever-increasing penetration of media in general and participatory media in particular:

From gaming to outdoor displays, performance to public transport, pervasive media is delivered into the fabric of everyday life, tuned to the context at the moment of delivery. It sits at the emerging intersection of mobile computers, media technology, networks and sensors and offers significant opportunities for new types of digital media content and services, especially those linked to an awareness of place and location.

(Pervasive Media Studio Website, 2011)

As participatory media become more and more a part of our daily lives, the requirement for self-representation is only likely to be extended. This means that all of the tensions in the processes of mediation shaping self-representation are both ever-more ubiquitous and ever-more urgently in need of analytical attention.

In this chapter I draw together the implications that arise from the empirical research presented in Chapters 4 and 5. In sections on institutional, cultural and textual processes of mediation, I consider what the particular dimension of mediation process might suggest about self-representation online. In each of the three sections I discuss the mediation of self-representation in general before turning to speculate about the particular case of Facebook.

As I write, it is announced that 'One in nine people now have a Facebook account as 750 million across the world have signed up to it' (*Telegraph*, 2011). No matter how reliable this exact figure, or what it masks in terms of type and kind of participation, it is nevertheless clear that the social networking site has fast become a global phenomenon. I focus on Facebook in this chapter because it serves to highlight the key tension in the mediation of self-representation online – ostensibly Facebook is about socialising and not about self-representation. But in order to participate in online socialising here, people *must* represent themselves. Thus self-representation is a condition of participation in this online space. On Facebook self-representation becomes both inadvertent and banal.[1]

Institutional mediation

Chapters 4 and 5 point to the complexity of the institutional dimension of mediation processes. A key area of tension in the processes of institutional mediation concerns the purposes of the projects within the institutions and the remit of the institutions themselves; for example, I explored how and why self-representation was invited by the BBC (Chapter 4) or the Arnolfini (Chapter 5). In turning to the self-representation taking place online I continue to be concerned with institutional processes of mediation. The question of whether platforms for self-representation are publicly funded or profit-driven, for example, and, crucially, to whom they are accountable, are key aspects of the processes of institutional mediation shaping any self-representation that takes place here. These are politically urgent questions when the role of public cultural institutions in facilitating self-representation is challenged by the argument that commercially run social media sites allow the creativity (including self-representation) of ordinary people on a massive scale and (it is claimed) subject to fewer processes of meditation.

The broader question of the role of public space in the online arena is an area of ongoing – and heated – debate in recent scholarly literature (e.g. Buckingham, 2010; Coleman and Blumler, 2009; Hartley, 2010; Jenkins, 2006). Jenkins' oft-cited concept of convergence culture included the convergence of public and commercial spaces. But Jenkins has also written of the limitations of participation in online spaces, limitations specifically arising from the commercial nature of many platforms (see Jenkins, 2007, on YouTube, below). On the other hand, John Hartley, taking up the idea of convergence culture, has argued that the received scholarly view, which regards public service space in a positive light and commercial space with suspicion, is rendered obsolete by developments in digital culture. Hartley argues that some of the most exciting and creative steps are being taken in commercial spaces (Hartley, 2010). David Buckingham (2010) insists that there remains a crucial need to maintain public spaces in the digital sphere. And Coleman and Blumler (2009) discuss the challenges involved in attempts to construct genuinely public spaces online.

That this wide-ranging debate is shaping the spaces actually existing at this very time is evidenced, for example, by recent policy and institutional developments – witness the BBC's recent decision (discussed in Chapter 4) to close many of its participatory, and oft-celebrated, online spaces (including those that have long facilitated self-representation like the *Video Nation* project) in favour of migrating such 'social' activities to commercial platforms like Facebook and Twitter which people already visit in much larger numbers than they ever visit BBC sites.[2]

It will not create stand-alone social networking sites, with any social propositions on the BBC site only there to aid engagement with BBC content. *The BBC will also ensure that its social activity works with external social networks.*

(BBC Strategy Review March, 2010, p. 57, my italics)

The commercial internet is the context to the majority of online self-representation, as Gripsrud reminds us: 'Most internet traffic these days is to sites owned and run by major institutions or corporations' (Gripsrud, 2010, p. 19).

YouTube, for example, is an institutional space that cannot be summed up by emphasising only one of the various kinds of practice which it enables, as Burgess and Green note,

In YouTube, new business models and more accessible tools of production are provoking new and uncertain articulations between alternative media and the mainstream, commercial media; and throwing up anxieties about issues of media authority and control. These uncertainties could partly explain the oscillation between two dominant explanatory frameworks for the website – YouTube as a player in the commercial new media landscape on the one hand (the top-down view), and YouTube as a site of vernacular creativity and lawless disruption on the other (the bottom-up view). [...] YouTube is not just another media company, and it is not just a platform for user-generated content.

(2009, p. 36)

Self-representation in commercial spaces may be mediated in ways which are less obvious but as important as the mediation evidenced in public service settings online. Moreover, in addition to considering publicly funded and commercial spaces, we also need to pay attention both to 'alternative' and to mainstream practices, *wherever they appear.* An analysis of how processes of institutional mediation shape self-representation in commercial settings must ask what the purposes of the self-representation in question are – that is to say, why it is taking place in a given setting. Moreover we should also consider how the political economic structures might actually shape the kinds of self-representation that take place in any given example. Finally, we need to ask how institutions construct the audience receiving the self-representations. Let us consider these questions in relation to the particular example of Facebook.

Institutional mediation in Facebook

In Facebook the same people are participants in and audience for self-representation – to be an audience for the self-representations of others, you must also represent yourself. The self-representing audience is thus shaped by the institution of Facebook by means of the idea that we should socialise online and do so with recourse to self-representations in image and text.

Once self-representations are being constructed, struggles over meaning ensue. Such struggles in the institutional mediation of self-representation highlight new versions of old problems about the possibilities and problems of representing others and the desire for self-representation.

Facebook is probably the most well-known social networking site in the world. A private company with headquarters in Palo Alto, California (Facebook, 2011), Facebook was established in 2004 and, according to the company's own statistics, 'reache[d] over 750 million active users' by July 2011 (ibid.). It is important to note that Facebook defines the contested notion of the 'active user' quite minimally as someone who has 'returned to the site in the last 30 days' (ibid.). In exploring the institutional processes of mediation shaping self-representation in Chapters 4 and 5 we have seen how a range of reasons in tension with each other combine to produce purposes for self-representation. When we look at self-representation in the social networking site Facebook, I suggest there are also tensions surrounding the purposes of the self-representation. In this case, the construction of a self-representation is a necessary, and unavoidable, aspect of taking part in social networking sites. Thus self-representation in Facebook is, very often at least, inadvertent, compared with the more considered examples we have met in previous chapters. Moreover, because it is an everyday aspect of participation, it is also banal.

Accepting this argument means we must revisit received understandings as to the key distinction between representation and self-representation. As we saw in Chapter 2, because it implies people representing themselves instead of being represented by others, self-representation carries with it a notion of *reduced mediation* because of the removal of the *mediators*. However, as I have been arguing, in instances of self-representation mediation is not removed, but rather the processes of mediation shape self-representations in ways that vary according to particular contexts and examples of the practice.

Now if self-representation is a necessary part of online socialising on a commercial platform such as Facebook, then it becomes clear that the idea that such a self-representation might be less mediated than any other, does not hold at all. Commercial interests frame the self-representation and aesthetic, moral and political decisions are made by people other than the person representing him or herself, just as with any other kind of representation (see the discussion of self-representation in Chapter 1). Thus the appearance of the Facebook page is heavily branded. Moreover this branding is not the white wall of the Museum of London web pages on which the thumbnails of the *16–19* project photographs were displayed, and by which they were framed as 'amateur content', as discussed in Chapter 5. Facebook is a highly recognisable commercial brand in colour, font and layout, and this branding, I suggest, is louder than any of the images or words that individuals upload to their profile pages. In addition to the strong brand of the company, advertising always lurks in the background; targeted advertisements appear in the same place on every page, that is, unless the individual user knows how to turn these off. Moreover, the owners of the company can sell users' information to a third party. In 2009, the following appeared across many Facebook 'walls' and similar postings have become a regular feature as privacy settings and commercial interests are continuously fought over:

IMPORTANT – *Facebook* has agreed to let a third party advertiser use your posted pictures without your permission. Click on SETTINGS up where you see the log out link. Select PRIVACY SETTINGS. Select NEWS FEEDS AND WALL. Select the tab that reads FACE BOOK ADS. There is a drop down box, select NO ONE. Save your changes. Please pass along.

The Facebook brand and multiple, changing and targeted adverts thus form part of any self-representation on Facebook – just as the white background constitutes a part of the self-representations produced for *London's Voices*.

Further examples that highlight struggles over self-representation in this setting include what kinds of language are allowed – while the list of languages in which Facebook is available is always expanding, nevertheless some languages dominate and some languages remain excluded. Moreover we can note the ways in which forms of censorship arise and are fought over, for example, the continuing campaign against the censorship of photographs featuring breastfeeding:

M.I.L.C. EVENT A HUGE SUCCESS!!!!!!!!!!!!!!!!!!!!!!!!!!!!

On December 27th, 2008 over 11 500 people participated in our first ever M.I.L.C. (Mothers International Lactation Campaign) event. Participants from around the globe joined our virtual protest of Facebooks discriminatory practice of arbitrarily and randomly removing breastfeeding pictures from member profiles and albums, classifying them as obscene content. We raised our collective voices in opposition to Facebook by posting a breastfeeding image as our profile picture and changing our status line to: Hey Facebook, breastfeeding is not obscene! In addition to our virtual nurse-in, a live nurse-in was held at Facebook headquarters in Palo Alto CA. Both events caught the attention of media world wide. Many members received warnings and had photos removed during and after the event. Some examples of these photos can be found here.[3]

Finally, we can consider the prioritising of particular technical developments over others as a form of institutional mediation in this setting, also subject to struggle. For example, in developing privacy controls the company must balance the needs of advertisers with those of the site's users. I suggest that all of these examples illustrate how struggles over self-representation, between the participants in Facebook and the owners of the company, are actually a banal aspect of participation in the site.

This sketch of the way in which institutional processes of mediation might shape self-representation in Facebook makes very clear that self-representation can never be free of mediation. Thus in this example, socialising is the foremost goal for the participant in, and user of, the site and profit-making is the ultimate goal for the company. But for both parties self-representation is an intrinsic part of what takes place. Self-representation in Facebook is just as institutionally mediated as it is in the other examples of self-representation that we have encountered in the preceding chapters.

Cultural mediation

The site, the purpose, the people represented and the kinds of representation produced are all crucially important to making sense of how processes of cultural mediation shape self-representation in the range of existing online spaces. Notwithstanding the particular commercial pressures in the institutional processes of mediation, it is nevertheless still the case that the processes of cultural mediation shaping self-representation in online spaces *not* run by established cultural institutions like broadcasting, museums and galleries are likely to be different to those which we have encountered in Chapters 4 and 5. Self-representation has become ubiquitous precisely because of the technological possibilities of the digital culture. Thus the kinds of input that the person who is representing him or herself can bring to bear are potentially far wider than anything we have encountered in the discussion of processes of cultural mediation in the preceding chapters. However we also know that, even of those connected to the internet, the number of people who are taking up the opportunity to represent themselves remains relatively low even in a wealthy country like the UK (e.g. Wardle and Williams, 2008).

The empirical material presented in Chapters 4 and 5 does make clear that what participants bring to the process of self-representation is always going to be absolutely key to making the self-representations what they are. Thus in a range of different contexts we have seen the undoing and redoing of the very concept 'ordinary person'. In *Capture Wales* and in *London's Voices* we have seen the explosion of the idea that there could be one purpose for self-representations. Meanwhile we have also observed that the range of *kinds* of self-representation in reality TV programming can be quite narrow. Moreover the resources necessary for mediating one's own self-representation might be precisely those that are lacking for the participants in reality TV programming – people must know how to represent both their authenticity (Coleman, 2006) and their ability to transform in the 'right' way (Skeggs, 2009). Thus, despite the fact that self-representations across these different spaces appear very alike – all being first-person accounts of experience – attending to the processes of cultural mediation highlights crucial differences across the range of self-representation in digital culture. In this section, analysis of self-representation online leads us to a combination of ideas about representation itself and debates about media literacy.

The ability to create is widely accepted as a key component of media literacy (Buckingham, 2010; Livingstone, Thumim and Van Couvering, 2005; Silverstone, 2007), and media literacy has become an increasingly central area of debate in contemporary media studies because participation requires literacy. A separate line of enquiry in media and cultural studies emphasises attending to questions of who is represented, who is not, but also which groups of people are only represented in certain settings or in particular and limited ways (e.g. Hall, 1997). I suggest that the combination of the concept of media literacy and the concept of representation take us to the heart of the processes of cultural mediation shaping self-representation in online spaces.

Whenever we encounter what looks like self-representation in online spaces we should be asking questions concerned with media literacy such as the following: how does this person know how to represent themselves, what has informed their decisions about how to represent themselves ('a strategy of representation' in Corner's terms (Corner, 1995a), discussed above), does this person try to secure an audience for their self-representation and if so how? These kinds of questions recall the Creative Director of *Capture Wales*, Daniel Meadows' emphasis on pedagogy, which was discussed in Chapter 4, that is, on teaching people how to use the tools with which they can most effectively represent themselves.[4] If self-representation is a necessary part of participation online, then the question of media literacy is possibly even more important than has already been generally accepted by scholars in the field.

A further line of enquiry suggested by the empirical work on self-representation presented in Chapters 4 and 5 would be to explore how notions of ordinary people are constructed, and how audiences *for* self-representation are shaped, in online settings. For example, YouTube appears to be the ultimate destination for the kinds of self-representation we have been exploring in previous chapters.

A self-representation on YouTube need not have been invited by the BBC or by a project at a public museum – thus the idea of *who* gets represented has the potential to be expanded beyond anything we have discussed in previous chapters and indeed YouTube has long been the site of apparently spontaneous self-representation. Potentially anyone can upload a video to YouTube and this might be a personal narrative, a political polemic or the airing of a perspective not often seen in the media, and it could therefore expand who we think is ordinary by challenging the idea that ordinariness must always be signalled by the representation of an experiential perspective. A YouTube self-representation does not rely on any particular educational strategy (unlike *Video Nation* or *Capture Wales*) nor is it necessarily edited by anyone other than the person representing him or herself (unlike *Faking It*, the Smithsonian Institute website *or Capture Wales*). And yet processes of cultural mediation must still always shape the self-representation in question – not least because the ability to upload the self-representation in general relies on the technical skill to do so.

A YouTube video might reach an audience of thousands or an audience of none. It might provoke pages of comments, 'reply videos', or none. As I write (July 2011), the top ten most watched YouTube videos are all commercial pop videos except *Charlie Bit My Finger* – a home movie in which a (white, American) baby bites his brother's finger. Moreover, as noted in Chapter 1, inequalities and prejudices are by no means absent from representation online. The question of who is represented and where and how they are represented remains problematic in the age of digital culture. Let us now return to the particular example of Facebook in order to explore the central tensions around media literacy and representation in processes of cultural mediation.

Cultural mediation in Facebook

Self-representation becomes more complicated and perhaps more urgently requires our attention precisely when representing oneself is *not* the primary objective. The use of the terms 'social media' and 'social network' emphasise the socialising aspect of the online arena and the remit of Facebook is not to facilitate self-representation by members of the public. Nevertheless I have suggested that self-representation is an unavoidable part of online socialising. We have briefly considered what might be some of the key constituents in processes of institutional mediation in Facebook. But clearly Facebook relies on its participants in order to be successful. Processes of cultural mediation are crucial in shaping self-representation in this setting as much as in the others we have encountered in previous chapters and we might expect to see a diversifying of the very idea of self-representation in a space in which the type of self-representation required is not explicitly specified by the institution.

When researching *Capture Wales*, I asked members of the production team if there was ever a digital story made that did not fulfil the brief and was not, therefore, displayed on the website. I was told that this rarely happened because the workshop process ensured the outcome was publishable, as noted in Chapter 4. The workshop process purposefully emphasised certain *kinds of* self-representation, namely first-person accounts of experience. There is nothing to prevent a person from using a photograph of someone else as their profile picture in Facebook; indeed many people use abstract images rather than the conventional self-portrait as their profile image. Moreover many Facebook users regularly change their visual self-representation. In this way Facebook profile pictures and status updates are often ephemeral. This ephemeral quality suggests that the processes of cultural mediation shaping self-representation might produce a diversification of kinds of self-representation. Thus, within the considerable strictures of the Facebook form (to which we will return) participants play with their own self-representation, using words and images, and changing these as often as they wish. Processes of cultural mediation are central in shaping what it is that participants decide to do – that is, how they choose to represent themselves.

Scholars discussing online social networking have repeatedly pointed to the blurring of boundaries between public and private communication in this arena (e.g. Bakardjieva, 2005). The fact that self-representation in Facebook takes place in a space whose publicness varies according to individual settings, for example, indicates the centrality of levels of media literacy to anyone's ability to control their own self-representation. Thus, while there may be the freedom to represent oneself by an abstract image one day and in fancy dress on another, there are nevertheless constraints which shape the self-representation and which are dependent on the degree of literacy the user has with the application itself. For example, I might post photographs of myself at a family party and intend to only share these personal images with close friends and yet, not understanding the privacy settings might make these images available to colleagues and acquaintances, or even to strangers. Moreover, even if one's settings are at the most private level, research suggests that privacy is a cause for concern among users of social networking sites (e.g. boyd, 2006). Rather than focusing on the question of the extent to which a platform such as Facebook is or is not private, perhaps we should take as given that social networking is not a private activity and, consequently, that self-representations that are produced in the process of social networking are also not private. This means that education in media literacy skills is of the utmost importance in order for Facebook users to understand the implications of their online socialising.

The term 'media literacy' is both widely and differently deployed. It is a highly contested concept with a history. Writing in 2008 about how different academic traditions (and political standpoints) have lately converged on this term, Sonia Livingstone, Elizabeth Van Couvering and myself favoured a social, cultural and political understanding of the term over a more individual, instrumental and regulatory one (see also Hartley, 2002):

> Media and information literacies do not simply concern the ability to access the electronic program guide for digital television or to complete one's income tax return online. Nor are the purposes restricted to becoming a more informed consumer or getting a higher paying job, though in methodological terms, these may be more readily evaluated against tangible outcomes. For literacy concerns the historically and culturally conditioned relationship between three processes: (a) the symbolic and material representation of knowledge, culture and values; (b) the diffusion of interpretative skills and abilities across a heterogeneous population; and (c) the institutional management (by public and private sector bodies) of the power that access to and skilled use of knowledge brings to those who are literate.
>
> (Livingstone, Van Couvering and Thumim, 2008, p. 126)

Management of online socialising requires administration and a degree of technical skill which many users lack. Thus people might publish postings as open to all their 'friends'. As a result, the postings will have a form and a character that the users are comfortable with presenting to all their Facebook friends who may be drawn from very different spheres of the individual's life. In this way media literacy contributes to the cultural mediation processes shaping self-representation in Facebook. It is clear that socialising and consequent self-representation in Facebook requires media literacy, which can help to deliver control over one's own representation, and this is arguably one of the reasons for its increasing centrality in media and communication in the era of digital ('social') media (e.g. Livingstone, Van Couvering and Thumim, 2005, 2008; Silverstone, 2007). The questions raised in relation to media literacy include the following – what kinds of media literacy skills are required in order for everyone who uses social networking to know how to operate available privacy settings, and moreover, to understand the extent (or lack thereof) of privacy such settings ensure? Referring to ethnographic work by Patricia Lange, Jean Burgess and Joshua Green make a related point in their study of YouTube:

> YouTube's vernacular producers attempt to control the 'publicness' of their participation in various ways, albeit with varying degrees of awareness of the extent to which relatively 'private' contributions might be accessed in ways outside their control (Lange 2007).
> (Burgess and Green, 2009)

Social networking requires a critical approach to content creation, specifically the developed ability to understand the way in which images are used in Facebook such that, for example, participation in social networking entails both the production of one's own self-representation and the acceptance that one may be represented by others. Moreover, because Facebook users routinely 'share' their photographs, images of a person may be visible to Facebook users, whether or not the person in the image is actually a Facebook user.

This is a different lack of control from that which ensues when a reality TV programme or a documentary is made about an individual, when media producers film, edit and display the individual representation, for example. However the fact that questions of media literacy come into play regarding the control over one's own self-representation suggests that, in addition to enabling and expansive opportunities for representing oneself, socialising in digital media spaces like Facebook leads to a new set of problems and constraints over self-representation from those that have been discussed in relation to older forms of media such as, for example, TV documentary.

Facebook and other social networking sites differ in many ways to the other kinds of self-representation we have encountered in previous chapters; a crucial difference is that the idea of a unitary self is defeated by the way the application works. The implications of this idea are enabling (you might represent yourself as a series of colours one week and as a working professional the next). However there is an extent to which you may be unable to control your own representations as these proliferate, change and are changed by others (e.g. Livingstone, 2008). The collective creation of ephemeral representations of individual selves may make us vulnerable to other people's portrayals of us, but at the same time might provide opportunities to play with the practice of self-representation and the idea of multiple identities.

Textual mediation

In Chapters 4 and 5 we saw that the processes of textual mediation included tensions over the idea of the ordinary person, the community, notions of quality and the purposes of the initiatives, whether in museums or the platforms used by broadcasters. It has been observed that much of what we encounter on YouTube, for example, is repurposed clips from mainstream media (e.g. Burgess and Green, 2009). However on YouTube we can also encounter self-representations which challenge dominant discourse sometimes through using and re-editing (e.g. Jenkins, 2006), sometimes through ignoring and sometimes through speaking back to mainstream media discourses and representations.

Friday Feminist Fuck You is an ongoing (occasional) series of to-camera short interventions on YouTube which are made by members of an American group called Feministing. The titles of some recent recordings indicate the kinds of topic addressed:

* *Friday Feminist Fuck You: Fox and Other Race-Dumb Outlets*
* *Friday Feminist Fuck You: Dr Laura*

- *Friday Feminist Fuck You: Anti-feminism in the media*
- *Friday Feminist Fuck You: Academy Awards*
- *Friday Feminist Fuck You: Grover Cleveland High.*

I want to note that these rejections of views represented in mainstream media are there to be stumbled across on YouTube in what are lately described by some scholars as 'postfeminist' times (e.g. McRobbie, 2009; Negra, 2009). Of course we should also note that the verbal comment 'responses', which are arguably just as important a part of YouTube as the videos to which they pertain, contain support and agreement as well as the misogyny you would expect to find. Mediation processes are power struggles. And these videos are buried in YouTube; they are not screened at the local multiplex. Nevertheless I suggest that videos like these should be taken as evidence of an explicit challenge to the fact that in dominant representations, as Negra rightly observes, 'the contemporary feminist [appears] as a narcissistic minority group member whose interests and actions threaten the family' (2009, p. 2). More broadly speaking, this example highlights the complexity of the various ways in which processes of textual mediation shape self-representation in online spaces.

Textual mediation in Facebook

Facebook is available in over 40 different languages and is thoroughly global in its structure, standing in contrast to national media such as newspapers and nationwide broadcasters. The technological infrastructure connects with both national and global communities, though of course the reality of people's online social worlds varies; some people will develop more international networks than others. Empirical sociological research indicates, for example, the prevalence of class inequality and the fixity of certain communities such as the white working class in England (e.g. Skeggs, 2004). Since online and offline worlds are interconnected, it is likely that less international offline worlds are also less international and cosmopolitan online as well, affecting what kinds of network people socialise in.

Debates about the individualisation thesis become relevant here (e.g. Beck, 1992; Giddens, 1991; Savage et al., 2001; Skeggs, 2004). Put simply, the individualisation thesis suggests that class identity is no longer a useful explanatory category for questions about identity formation in a globalised world (despite the 'continued existence of class inequalities'). Savage et al. explain,

> These writers argue that the contemporary weakness of class identities indicates that we are in a period of major social and cultural change that has moved us on beyond the paradigm of the class societies of capitalist-industrial society. The idea of the end of class is one of the few unifying themes that these various accounts of the rise of postmodern, post-industrial, postFordist and late modern societies share. It might be pointed out that despite the fact that all the writers listed above recognise, and at times (notably Beck 1992) emphasise the continued existence of class inequalities, none of them is able to provide a convincing account of how material social inequalities relate to identity formation
>
> (2001, pp. 876–7).

Meanwhile other sociologists argue that the individualisation theory actually serves to normalise a particular worldview and deny the experience of those who are not mobile, global selves (Skeggs, 2004). Thus while Facebook's stated mission is 'Giving people the power to share and make the world more open and connected',[5] Facebook networks are likely to mirror the social networks of everyday life; if these are not global and mobile, then neither will a particular person's online network be.

There are opportunities to bring all aspects of the individualised self into this online space, so when the individual identifies with a politics, then politics can be present. Thus the 'group' Get the Fascist BNP off Facebook is a good example (as is the British National Party (BNP) being on Facebook in the first place for that matter). This group is listed under a hyperlink: 'Common Interest – Beliefs and Causes' (Facebook website). Thus, in this framing, group politics emerges from, and belongs to, individual Beliefs and Causes (a sub-section of Common Interest). Another group in this section is entitled 'I flip my pillow over to get to the cold side'. Thus in Facebook framing anti-fascist politics is equivalent to what you do with your pillow in bed – a matter of personal, individual taste as to whether it matters or whether it is a joke, not a group cause for action. Similarly, the expressions of opinion about Barak Obama's candidacy can also be read as delivering a particular type of self-representation. The architecture of Facebook – the status update in this case – encourages expressions of individual feeling in not more than two sentences and hence, in this illustration, reaction to the election in this illustration comes across as a collection of individual feelings, although we should also note that Facebook, just like YouTube (Burgess and Green, 2009), is used in more than one way and for more than one purpose. Social networking sites *are* used to build offline political actions (e.g. Fenton, 2007) – witness the UK riots of 2011 and the subsequent community 'clean ups', both of which reportedly used social networking to communicate.

All kinds of commercial outlet (grocers, fashion companies, weight-loss companies, health clubs, computer companies) now invite customers to ' "like" us on Facebook' (and 'follow us on Twitter'). The invitation to 'Get The Fascist BNP off Facebook', the statement that 'I flip my pillow over to get to the cold side' and the information that I 'like' 'Painted Lady Hairdressing Salon' all contribute to how I represent myself on Facebook – so that shopping, politics, fashion and what I do to my pillow are all equivalent parts of the identity I am representing.

The common-sense assumption is that Facebook is primarily a tool for socialising and yet profile pictures do largely consist of amateur portrait snaps and the website is set up explicitly to upload and 'share' photos of 'me'. This means creating representations of 'me'. And it is only once we think about the self-representation that *must* take place *in order* to socialise in Facebook that we are able to address the important question of how these representations interact with dominant media representations. – that is, do they challenge them, ignore them, uphold them or alter them?

Facebook is a website designed to elicit certain responses, that is, certain kinds of representation. When our images are posted there they take on the Facebook brand, which provides the gallery space, if you will, for photographs, thoughts and other kinds of position-taking. Perhaps one of the most striking features of mediated self-representation in Facebook is the focus on the individual self, which follows the trajectory discussed above, which has taken place in, for example, the Access movement and documentary production more widely. Stories of the self have always been told (think of diaries, letters, the history of family photography) but in Facebook (and

Facebook is only one example of social networking) these practices are in the service of socialising, networking, staying in touch. What kind of photograph of yourself do you post? Which image represents you, today, in this mood, at this moment, how are you feeling? Even the most professional images look snapshot-like, 'amateur' here because of the overbearing and very familiar frame of the Facebook brand. When an individual wants to socialise in Facebook they post images of themselves, stories of their mood, their opinion, their feelings onto the Facebook site and in so doing they are conforming to what we can see as the *generic expectations* of the self-representation, an idea to which I return in Chapter 7.

Conclusion

It should now be clear that we will have to abandon the idea that self-representation online is less mediated than it is in other settings where it may come about for all sorts of varied reasons, as we have seen. Self-representation in the spaces of Web 2.0, such as YouTube, Facebook and Twitter, is subject to different tensions in the processes of institutional, textual and cultural mediation than self-representation in the platforms provided by broadcasters, by museums or by art galleries. In short, self-representation is *not ever* free of mediation, but it *is always* mediated differently in different settings, as Corner reminds us,

> The web has emerged as a public space, a counter-public space, a private space, a popular space, a market space and (to some degree) a state space, with various and shifting configurations between these aspects as they affect localized profiles.
>
> (2009, p. 147)

My argument in this chapter has been that while the particular tensions constituting the processes of mediation may be different in relatively new online spaces to those in the spaces run by long-established cultural institutions of various kinds, they are, by definition, never entirely removed. Indeed, invited self-representation, such as that which took place in *Capture Wales* or *London's Voices*, might be freer, in some ways, than that which occurs in some of the other kinds of space in the participatory web where self-representation is a condition of participation. The strength of a focus on mediation is that it highlights the whole, messy range of perspectives that contribute to the meaning of self-representation.

It should now also be clear that processes of mediation in and of themselves are neither 'good' nor 'bad' and hence a more pure, more true, morally superior self-representation will never be reached as the result of the promise that processes of mediation can be reduced. The idea that processes of mediation can be reduced is, in my view, a misunderstanding of what processes of mediation are and how they must always work to shape the meaning of representations. Rather than processes of mediation ever being reduced, what I have established and illustrated in these last three chapters is that the possibilities and constraints arising from the ways in which self-representation is mediated in different settings echoes the possibilities, constraints and tensions surrounding cultural forms in general (e.g. Corner, 2009). Moreover the conceptual separation of the three dimensions of the mediation processes emphasises the need to consider how exactly institutional and industrial structures *intersect* with textual forms and cultural participations.

The analytical work presented in this book suggests the need for spaces for self-representation that deal explicitly with challenges in literacy and representation. Perhaps this is why scholars and practitioners in a range of formal and informal institutions across the world return repeatedly to digital storytelling as a distinctive and politically important model among the proliferating and widely diverse examples of self-representation that take shape and circulate more or less fleetingly in digital culture:

> There are many ways to make media and many reasons for making it. The Center's work is guided by a strong commitment to offering non-threatening production environments in which the process of creating digital work is just as meaningful as the stories created. We support the individual learning styles of workshop participants rather than insisting on uniform methods, we stress the importance of understanding why and how stories are being produced, and we encourage our storytellers and collaborating partners to share their stories in ways that support positive individual and collective change.[6]
>
> (Center for Digital Storytelling, 2011)

This excerpt from the Center for Digital Storytelling website, Berkeley, California, is particularly interesting for the ideas I have been exploring because of its focus on production process. The analysis I have presented of self-representation in diverse settings, shows that we cannot hope to make sense of textual self-representations that appear to be alike unless we look behind them into their construction, by exploring their processes of institutional and cultural mediation. Yet we must address the fact that they nevertheless *do* look alike, that is, that we can now speak of the *genre* of self-representation being deployed in politically and socially different ways in different settings. Chapter 7 explores the argument for conceptualising self-representation as a genre across the range of spaces in which it is encountered and addresses the question of what kinds of work this genre is doing.

7
Self-Representation, Digital Culture and Genre

Introduction

How might we address the paradox by which the self-representations circulating in contemporary digital culture can appear alike and yet be completely different in what they mean and how they are valued? I suggest that we need two concepts: mediation and genre. In this chapter I propose that a genre of self-representation has emerged through the analysis in the preceding pages. And yet there are myriad differences in what kinds of work different examples of this genre seem to be doing. I have suggested that a critical exploration of self-representation must address theories of representation (the analysis of texts), but that it must go beyond the analysis of texts to explore both the production of self-representation and the cultural contexts of participants. In the case of self-representation, accounting for production and cultural contexts as well as paying attention to texts enables us to distinguish between examples of self-representation that may look alike at a textual level but that arise in entirely different production contexts, for different purposes, involving different processes of production and engaging different 'ordinary people'. In short, analysis of the three dimensions of mediation process foregrounds the question of the value of different examples of the genre of self-representation and enables us to address the question of how the genre of self-representation is being used – what work it is doing and in whose interests.

Drawing on theoretical debate about the turn to the concept of mediation, I have suggested that it is through processes of mediation that any particular self-representation is constituted. Thus in order to understand the meaning and, consequently, to speculate about the value of self-representations, a conceptual framework consisting of three dimensions of mediation process was proposed – namely institutional, textual and cultural processes of mediation. I have shown how it is that meaning-making takes place through and across these three dimensions of the mediation process, enabling us to make sense of ubiquitous and unlike self-representation albeit with one important caveat – an analysis of the reception of self-representations would further expand (and complicate) the processes of cultural mediation in this model. I return to this point below. This final chapter is in two parts. In the first part the notion of a genre of self-representation is proposed as the key to apprehending the alikeness of self-representations. In the final part I draw on the three dimensions of mediation to ask how the *genre* of self-representation might be useful in theory and in practice.

Self-representation and genre

In the preceding chapters I have positioned textual analysis of individual self-representations as a key element in understanding the dimension of the mediation process that I have been calling textual mediation. Because textual analysis in general is a contested form of analysis within the multidisciplinary and overlapping field of media studies, film studies, and media and communications, we need first to address the debate over textual analysis in general, before moving on to explore the particular problems that are raised by a textual analysis of self representation by 'ordinary people'. Let us discuss these two ideas before moving into a discussion of the genre of self-representation that includes, but is not only concerned with, texts.

The very usefulness of textual analysis to understanding media has long been cause for debate across the multidisciplinary field of media and communication, and this is a discussion that shows no sign of abating (see, for example, Corner, 1995b; Couldry, 2000b). As Corner argues, the debate revolves around different understandings of knowledge in the arts and social sciences (Corner, 1995b). In the arts evidence takes the form of a convincing (and well-supported) argument; in the social sciences evidence should be drawn

from empirical data rather than what is seen to be the opinion of a
lone scholar:

> The arts and social science combination in Media Studies is essen-
> tially one which brings together 'criticism' and 'sociology' as
> modes of academic knowing. Criticism is a mode privileging indi-
> vidual percipience, in which knowledge is the product of sustained
> analytic attention and intellection. It has a direct, informing link
> with 'opinion' and, indeed, it is 'opinion' rather than ' theory'
> as such which is its main generator of ideas. That such opinion
> is, by definition, subjective (often deeply and self-declaredly so)
> is by no means a drawback to the larger project of intercritical
> activity (characterized as 'debate') In literary studies, for instance,
> a powerfully rendered account of a major novelist may be prized
> for its 'originality', precisely for the way in which it differs from
> the interpretations made by other people. [...] Sociology, on the
> other hand, in its classic and defining empirical project, is essen-
> tially a mode privileging method. However cautiously it relates
> itself to (or distances itself from) natural science paradigms, the
> production of knowledge is normatively regulated by the use of
> procedures which are explicit, in line with intersubjective agree-
> ments on validity (even if these are only partial) and able to be
> replicated by those who wish to 'test' findings. What the pro-
> cedures produce is, first of all, 'data', and then an analysis and
> explanation of this data. Both data and the analyses which are
> made of it (the two should not be confused) have a very different
> status from 'criticism'.
>
> (Corner, 1995b, pp. 148–9)

Thus the argument in a social sciences approach to media and communication asks why a given interpretation of a text is *the* right one,
or truer than any other, while arts approaches to media and communication are precisely interested in offering convincing 'readings'.
In exploring self-representation in digital culture in the preceding
pages I have drawn on social science and arts approaches to media
and communications – both are important to making sense of the
mediation processes that shape self-representation. However the contested nature of the 'evidence' produced by textual analysis must be
acknowledged.

A group of several teenagers participated in the workshop that produced the poem 'Mr Transitional' (discussed in Chapter 5); indeed, other poems produced in that workshop appeared on the Museum of London's *16–19* website under the same title. Furthermore, the writing workshops were just one of the kinds of activity that participants across London took part in as part of the *London's Voices 16–19* projects. Two groups of young people produced photographs, and the photograph by 'Kimberley' that is discussed in Chapter 5 was just one of the photographs that 'Kimberley' took that were displayed on the project website. Moreover, *16–19* was just one of eighteen subprojects making up *London's Voices*. Dai Evans' digital story *My Two Families* (discussed in Chapter 4) is just one among hundreds of digital stories produced and displayed on the *Capture Wales* websites. And, of course, *Capture Wales* and *London's Voices* are just two examples among many in which people are producing self-representations. In the end the choice of which particular 'text' (self-representation) to explore through textual analysis must be subjective, if not random. Given the current ubiquity of such texts, we might be satisfied with such sampling, but must also bear it in mind in evaluating the overall findings.

The research explored in the preceding chapters does not allow us to know to what extent the various self-representations produced are popular with audiences – audience response to the self-representations discussed has not been explored. Moreover, it seems odd to subject self-representations to an analysis that takes them seriously in terms of form, content and narrative. Are not these just snapshots of daily life or elements within a broader programme? Do all kinds of self-representation really warrant serious critical attention? The question becomes – what is the use of textual analysis? It seems to me that the discomfort raised – the very oddness encountered in producing textual analyses of self-representations – is itself important. This discomfort is actually revealing about the processes of mediation shaping self-representations.

Firstly, my discomfort shows that I take on the division which situates the self-representations discussed in the preceding pages as 'amateur', not professional, content and that this division is a hierarchical one – professional content deserving critical attention, whereas the purpose of amateur content is something else and that content is therefore not supposed to be read in the same way. Yet analysis reveals tensions in the texts themselves, for example, between the photograph taken by a participant in *16–19* and its setting on the professionally branded Museum of London website.

Secondly, the idea of the ordinary is raised by this discomfort. If these self-representations are by, and of, 'ordinary people', then the implication is that they must be interchangeable and it does not matter which are chosen to be looked at in detail. And yet, a sustained analysis of any example always highlights the fact that these self-representations are each unique and so troubles the categorisation 'ordinary'. An illustration of this is the example discussed in Chapter 4 in which the young participant in *Faking It* tearfully exclaims to camera 'I mean, yeah, maybe I don't not know what I like but I f*** know what I hate and this is what I hate'. At the same time, the framing of self-representations like this by the institutions shows them as representations of 'ordinary people' – of whom there are always, by definition, many more. If we look at self-representations by professionals – artists and documentary makers – we might also find the category 'ordinary' is being problematised.

Thirdly, the idea of community is raised. Should these individual self-representations be plucked from their framing as part of a community? Do they make sense on their own, out of that context? The discomfort I encountered in producing these textual analyses suggests that some of the sense of what these self-representations are is lost when they are taken out of the communal context in which they are always displayed. And yet the analysis of micro- and macro-texts, and the relationship between them, reveals tensions about the idea of community.

Fourthly, how can the fact that individual self-representations are moving – that is why they work – be conveyed and understood, without a detailed exploration of what they consist of in terms of form, content and narrative? How the self-representations are made and how the issue of value – of the person represented and of the representation itself – is implicated in the answers to these questions is key to the processes of mediation shaping self-representations.

Each self-representation across digital culture could be subjected to the same close reading that I have given to the various examples discussed in the preceding chapters. In each one, the detail provided leads to a deconstruction of the notion of the 'ordinary person' that has at the same time been constructed using the generic conventions of the self- representation. Considering the mediation of self-representation as being concerned with the idea of value, we can turn to the notion of genre as a way of making sense of ubiquitous self-representations. For what is always striking about self-representations is the 'amateur aesthetic' on which they rely and which invokes both celebration and derision. Perhaps the amateur is always linked to the idea of authenticity, and both with the genre of self-representation. To explore this idea we need to use a more expansive definition of 'genre'.

Genre and the generic

The concept of genre is both contested and deceptively simple, because the term exists in everyday speech to refer to types, and across disciplines and fields of practice, it is used in a range of more complicated ways. Genre in everyday speech, as Altman and Neale have both observed, refers to types of thing, but academic use of the notion of genre is (of course) more complicated, and more interesting (Altman, 1999; Neale, 2000).

Literary genres do not map neatly onto cinematic ones or those used in the scholarly field of film criticism. Genre in film studies is another related, but nevertheless distinct, field of debate with a particular history largely focused on Hollywood cinema.

Here we see in-depth critical debates about genre and the generic. All of this follows from an earlier moment in film studies which focused on the *auteur* and the move to a discussion of genre was to some extent an attempt to take into account rather than to avoid (as *auteur* theory had done) the conditions of production. Genre theory is thus clearly and explicitly linked to debates about quality and value specifically as these arise from *industrial* (and, we might say in the context of this study, *institutional*) production processes. And notions of value and quality are, as we have seen in previous chapters, absolutely key to making sense of the genre of self-representation.

Within the field of media and communications, some of the controversy and debate over value is absent from discussion of genre and here genre is more about distinguishing different types. The type, crucially, is not based on the text alone, but also on communication between producers and the audiences who make meaning from texts. Understandings of genre in the field of media and communications/media studies have been explained as a contract between producers and audiences, as Chandler summarised: 'Genres can be seen as constituting a kind of tacit contract between authors and readers' (1997, p. 6).

It is also commonplace in media and communications and the study of broadcast TV to hear reference to genre hybridity. Reality TV and popular factual programming have long been designated as hybrid genres, endlessly recombining elements of other genres (see Mast, 2009; Piper, 2004; Skeggs et al., 2008). Thus we hear reference to genres and sub-genres and to hybrid genres. I suggest that in all of these examples the conception of genre as a contract may still hold; I argue that it does. We know what an abstract photograph is because of a tacit understanding between producer and audience. We know now that reality TV will, by definition, combine familiar genres (the game show, the drama, the observational documentary). Now I suggest that another genre which is combined with these others in reality TV and elsewhere (as explored in the preceding chapters) is the genre of self-representation. The idea that a genre is based on a tacit understanding or a contract is helpful. Moreover this notion of tacit understanding allows us to consider self-representation as a genre that appears across fields of practice and scholarship – such as the multiple sites apprehended in this book. Audiences know self-representation when they see it. Or do they?

If a genre appears in multiple settings all with different contexts of production and reception and textual form, we need to consider (a) what unites these disparate examples and (b) if there is a genre of self-representation, what work this genre is doing. This question takes us to the heart of the issue of why it is useful to use the concept of genre to think about self-representation across sites that are unlike each other in so many ways. To put it another way – how and why does the concept of genre help us to make sense of ubiquitous self-representation?

For several years now scholars have been attending to the increasingly common blurring of boundaries between factual and entertainment genres on TV. Hill et al. (2007) have suggested that audiences *use* genre to make sense of a changing factual media environment and specifically to make sense of programmes which combine elements of genres that have, as Corner has noted, historically been associated with public knowledge on the one hand and popular culture on the other (Corner, 1991, 2009). Hill et al. observe,

Viewers use genre evaluation as a tool for understanding a wide range of factual content. Television viewing trends for contemporary news, documentary and reality programming show a genre map divided according to pre existing categories associated with public knowledge and popular culture. This way of categorising and valuing factual and reality programmes highlights the importance of social and generic discourses on television, and preexisting attitudes towards British and Swedish television contexts and genres.

> (Hill et al., 2007, p. 18)

Hill et al.'s survey of British and Swedish audiences shows these audiences to be adept at deciphering the different elements in these hybrid genres. That is to say, audiences are media literate, contra to some of the indications in earlier reviews of the research literature in this area (Livingstone and Thumim, 2003, Livingstone et al., 2005). Hill et al.'s research thus suggests an improvement in audience literacy as audiences have become accustomed to these hybrid genres.

Their discussion both highlights the role of audiences in making genres and suggests that the hybridisation of broadcast genres has become normal. Moreover they note: 'Viewers do not experience news or documentary or reality TV in isolation but as part of factuality as a whole' (ibid.). I want to emphasise the argument made here that viewers do not experience genres *in isolation* and I take this point further – members of the public do not experience broadcast genres in isolation, instead they experience them as part of their mediated lives. As recent audience research has emphasised, people are not only viewers; the same people view broadcast TV, surf the internet and encounter the projects carried out by museums and galleries, for example. People are (at least) both audiences and publics (Livingstone, 2005b).

As explored in the preceding chapters we now encounter self-representation across a range of sites. I suggest that we are seeing the genre of self-representation being *used* in different hybrid forms within these settings. But how can such different examples all be examples of the genre of self-representation? We do not want to say that self-representation in BBC Wales' *Capture Wales* is the same as self-representation in *Faking It* or that either of these are the same as self-representation in *Facebook*. Moreover works of autobiography by fine artists such as video work by Tracy Emin are different again. Yet I do want to argue that these are all examples of the genre of self-representation. How, then, am I using genre in a way that can allow me to make the argument that these diverse examples are all instances of the genre of self-representation, while still acknowledging their various and crucial differences including political, social and cultural purpose?

Genre as cultural artefact

In a 2002 overview of overlapping and distinct theories of genre, film scholar Steve Neale notes that, despite debates, theorists agree that 'genre is a multi-dimensional phenomenon' (Neale, 2000, p. 25). And in a 2002 introduction to an edited collection of new work on genre and contemporary Hollywood, he notes,

> Genres can be approached from the point of view of the industry and its infrastructure, from the point of view of their aesthetic traditions, from the point of view of the broader socio-cultural environment upon which they draw and into which they feed, and from the point of view of audience understanding and response.
>
> (Neale, 2002, p. 2)

A review around the same time, in 1999, of debates and developments in genre practice and theory, led the film scholar Robert Altman to note,

> Generic intertextuality has increased in importance so that the media can offer viewers a new 'home' located in previous media-viewing experiences and the comfort of recognizing generic references.
>
> (1999, p. 194)

According to two of its leading theorists, then, contemporary genre is both multidimensional and intertextual. I suggest that the genre of self-representation is a case in point: people *encounter* the generic conventions of self-representation that are *produced* as different kinds of text and displayed in a range of settings.

Altman is specifically concerned with genre in film, but his idea (above) that genre provides 'home' and comfort is a productive one for our discussion. He continues,

> It hardly surprises me to note the rapid rise of generic thinking over the past decade or so. The technological and representational explosion of recent years only reinforces earlier patterns of alienation and lost presence. In this atmosphere, genre can easily appear to represent a safe harbour in which to ride out the storm.
>
> (1999, p. 194)

Let us now consider specifically self-representation as a multidimensional and intertextual genre (institution, text, culture) that offers the 'familiar' and the 'safe'.

Through Chapters 4–6 we have explored the activity of self-representation in different sites. We looked at the engagement in activities of self-representation by broadcasters, the activity of self-representation in museum and art worlds, and the activity of self-representation online. In these chapters we looked at ordinary members of the public speaking for themselves in these different settings – moreover, *making* representations of themselves, rather than being represented by others. Thus we have seen opportunities for ordinary people to 'speak for themselves' in all of these sites; we have see the invitation to people to take up an opportunity to speak for themselves and we have seen their involvement in the production of their self-representations.

The genre of self-representation

In this section I attempt to gather together what might be characteristics of a recognisable genre of self-representation. Those characteristics which mean this is a genre in that sense of a tacit agreement, that is to say a contract between producers and audiences. The characteristics of the genre of self-representation include combinations of some or all of the following elements:

- ordinary people
- ordinary people located in community
- community

- emotion
- experience
- interior worlds
- personal history
- idea of a personal 'journey' (actual or metaphorical)
- individual perspective
- any voice-over is in the first person
- speaking to camera in close-up
- home-made, DIY, scrapbook, aesthetics
- family photographs
- personal artefacts.

The truth claims of authentic photographs discussed by John Ellis (2010) link to the status of self-speaking as the accepted, indeed the righteous, position and this is a part of what makes the genre of self-representation cohere. If, as Ellis observes, '[A]ny broadcast text is an assemblage of communicative attempts' (2010, p. 192), then this self-representation involves the attempt to persuade of the authenticity of the ordinary person's point of view. I suggest that there is such a thing as a recognisable (and multidimensional) genre of self-representation. Secondly, I am arguing that examples of this genre are different in their politics, purpose, conditions of production and more, and that in attending to processes of mediation we can see what these differences are. Moreover we can then ask what kinds of self-representation the proliferating examples we encounter today might be.

Mediation and the uses of the genre of self-representation

Despite diverse processes of mediation, what we have been looking at across the range of examples discussed is still self-representation, and hence Altman's notion of an intertextual genre is useful. I am using it in an even broader sense than Altman (a film scholar) may have intended, but my interest is in the analytical usefulness of the notion of genre for highlighting that self-representation takes a recognisable form across a range of (more or less intersecting) sites in the cultural spheres of everyday life. The genre of self-representation is not limited to reality TV, to social networking, to public service broadcasting, to the outreach projects of museums and artists. The genre of self-representation, of course, includes many cases that I have *not* focused on in the preceding pages. Thus the genre of self-representation includes the work of professional artists and film-makers as well as that of 'ordinary people' in innumerable settings across the net, from the more well-known YouTube first-person videos to the less well-known, niche and even hidden examples of self-representation. Indeed the genre of self-representation (as with other genres) must include examples which self-consciously play with key features of the genre including the authentic, the experiential and the very boundary between professional and amateur.

And yet in the cases I have explored the analysis of the three dimensions of mediation through which the self-representations are constituted shows that while these self-representations may often *look* the same, they are not the same. Thus self-representations must be made sense of as precisely multidimensional phenomenon (in Neale's terms) so that we can argue about the difference between self-representation in *Faking It* and self-representation in *Capture Wales*, self-representation on YouTube and self-representation within the walls of Tate Modern. Only then can we enter into the thorny and fascinating terrain of questions of value and politics in diverse examples of the genre.

I have established that it is not useful to speak of degrees of mediation in the sense of a self-representation on Facebook being unmediated and a reality TV self-representation being heavily mediated. Instead, I argue that, since self-representation is always mediated, the three dimensions of institutional, textual and cultural mediation enable us to address in detail the question of how these processes of mediation work for any example. Thus we can see that a self-representation in a *Capture Wales* digital story is shaped by the strictures of the digital storytelling form as developed first at the Center for Digital Storytelling in Berkeley, California and then in the New Media Department at BBC Wales, by the institutional tensions surrounding the decisions to fund, facilitate and display self-representations by members of the BBC's audience, and by the competencies, expectations, skills and voices of the participants themselves. A self-representation on Channel Four's *Faking It* is required as a vital constituent of what audiences and producers now expect from reality TV participation and the programme also requires the intimate to-camera address by the star of each episode. In some accounts self-representation in reality TV is not voluntary, but rather demanded (e.g. Skeggs, 2009). Moreover such self-representation forms part of a programme edited by media professionals, which, whether on commercial or public service channels, is there to entertain and engage large numbers of viewers. The self-representation facilitated by the Arnolfini, Knowle West Media Centre and Suzanne Lacy uses ordinary people to provoke discussion of received ideas about the value of those people's skills and knowledge in society – but also contributes to debates within the field of fine art about what constitutes such art. In short, it is clear that understanding the genre of self-representation is only possible when mediation processes are taken into account. This same analysis, I suggest might usefully be applied to other examples both those at the heart and those at the edges of the genre.

The concept of three dimensions of mediation contributes both to understanding of self-representation and to debates about the concept of mediation itself. In Chapters 4–6 I have explored how self-representations are shaped by three dimensions of mediation. This discussion has made clear both the importance of the different dimensions in meaning-making and the diversity in self-representations that at first sight may appear alike. Nevertheless the separation of mediation processes into three dimensions is a conceptual and not an actual one. In practice, of course, these dimensions combine to shape the genre of self-representation.

The range of institutional contexts in which self-representation is currently being produced includes commercial TV companies and stations, advertising agencies, social media companies, public service broadcasters, museums, art galleries, charities and development organisations, as well as other kinds of public and private organisations that are not traditionally seen as cultural producers (global corporations, and national health services, for example).

The examples explored in this book suggest that the institutional processes of mediation are likely to include tensions over the very purpose of self-representation in any given example. If an organisation deploys digital storytelling, the precise purposes for carrying out that activity are likely to differ for the various people involved in the process, particularly where the organisation is a large and diverse one, such as the BBC in Wales, for example.[1] The detailed qualitative research at BBC Wales, discussed in Chapter 4, illustrates how tensions over purposes contribute to processes of institutional mediation in this BBC project and different tensions around purpose emerge when artists and art galleries work with self-representation, as we saw in Chapter 5. Very different kinds of tension about purpose mediate self-representation online. Self-representation online spans the quite banal and often inadvertent condition of online socialising, as we saw in Chapter 6, the now well-established practice of first-person video found on YouTube and the practice of film-makers and artists who display work online (Burgess and Green, 2009; Dovey and Rose, 2012).

I suggest that the construct 'ordinary people' informs and shapes the institutional processes of mediation shaping self-representation that exist for diverse purposes and in the range of quite different contexts which we have explored in the preceding chapters. The analysis has suggested that the idea of 'ordinary people' does invoke the negative, denigratory connotations of Adorno and Horkheimer's undifferentiated, ignorant and even threatening, label 'mass'. Indeed, in some cases the producers' understanding of that connotation informs their reluctance to use the term or, if they do use it, then they qualify it to indicate their awareness of the problems it raises.

We have seen how participants in projects inviting people to represent themselves were offhand about the possibility of their self-representations appearing in public settings, we have also seen self-representation occurring as a kind of banal by-product of socialising online. Nevertheless the unequal power relationship between the institutions and the participating audience is structural – it is hard to see how it could be avoided – across the examples discussed.[2] This does suggest that the media institutions themselves remain central to the processes of mediation shaping self-representation. And while a process of disintermediation (Katz, 1988) may be taking place by virtue of the fact that members of the audience (or 'the people formerly known as the audience' (Rosen, 2006)) are in a position to create media in unprecedented ways, nevertheless, there are audiences encouraged and assisted in the creation of media representations who might not be doing so without the facilitation of institutions. There is a role for professionals as facilitators, then, but this also means that disintermediation does not adequately explain the processes I have explored; the institutions still retain the power to frame representations – even when the institution in question is a private company like Facebook and not a public service broadcaster like the BBC. Moreover, we have seen how new intermediaries take on important roles in communicating across diverse platforms and between groups of people and institutions.

The dimension of processes of textual mediation shows us a deceptively simple aspect (we can gather together the characteristics of a self-representation (see the section on genre of self representation above), but as soon as we look at micro- and macro-texts any illusion of simplicity is destroyed. The micro-text of the self-representation in the macro-context of the website at the Museum of London is an example – or the micro-context of the to-camera diary room moment that is so central to *Big Brother* in the macro-context of the entire *Big Brother* episode; or the micro-context of the washing powder advertisement in the macro-context of a set of programmes that are an advertisement break in, for example, the soap opera, *Coronation Street*; or the micro-text, and fleeting, profile photo and status update, in the news feed encountered by a Facebook user. The technology of the internet interface makes possible a particular framing – a framing which, I have argued, clearly evidences tensions over the sometimes conflicting – even contradictory – purposes of the self-representations. The aesthetics developed with the digital technology are central to the 'amateur' aesthetic by which we recognise self-representation as such. But this use of new technology also relies heavily on a longer history of 'amateur aesthetic' which used earlier technologies of cut and paste, for example (Atton, 2002).

The very idea of *using* new technologies is a central part of the mediation of self-representation across the range of examples encountered in the preceding chapters and that this is consistently present confirms the critical importance of the discussions of fear, desire and imagination when it comes to the subject of new media and new technology, as discussed in Chapter 1.

Producers of *Capture Wales*, run by the New Media department of BBC Wales, specifically set out to use new media technologies in innovative ways. Similarly the overall aim of *London's Voices* was to broaden access to the already existing Oral History Collection and to experiment with new ways of collecting. New technologies were seen to be integral to these goals in absolutely concrete ways: *Capture Wales* developed the digital storytelling form as a way to connect with audiences and to deliver new content for the BBC websites; *London's Voices* made parts of its archive available on the web, collected new contributions from members of the audience through using new technology for collecting, and used the internet to display the newly collected self-representations. The Facebook company is explicitly concerned with developing and promoting the use of this interactive, social tool in order to promote a certain kind of socialising – to make a successful (and profitable) product – in order to deliver an audience to an advertiser.

Meanwhile, on the part of the people who represent themselves, we have seen panic about how to use new technology, excitement and dread about what it might mean, as well as a complete lack of interest in the technological aspects of their activity. Other examples of self-representation not explored in this volume will likely show further attitudes to technology such as the promise seen by those working in a documentary tradition (Dovey and Rose, forthcoming). A range of attitudes to technology are evident across the range of sites of self-representation explored in the preceding pages, from the apparent belief in the intimacy of a to-camera moment in a reality TV show that will be broadcast to thousands to the nonchalance about the idea that anyone would ever even view a digital story about a garden shed in Wales. Interviews suggest that participants imagine audiences with whom they communicate across time and space – that is to say, they consider both geographically separated audiences and audiences in the future. Such imaginings are possible because of the fact that self-representations are constructed using digital technologies and displayed on websites promising both indefinite preservation and global access.

It is not surprising to find that the persons involved in the day-to-day production of self-representations produced in museums, galleries and artist- and community-based projects want to claim that there is a value in enabling the production and display of ordinary people's self-representations. What kind of value this is, however, is not straightforward, and I shall return to this point.

For the institutions, the facilitation of self-representation contributes to their legitimacy today. Excluded voices are given a space on institutional platforms and in this process these accounts are rendered legitimate as alternative versions of history and of the contemporary. Such processes emerge in the facilitation of self-representation undertaken by the Arnolfini and the Smithsonian Institute, as discussed in Chapter 5. They are clear in Huw Davies', a Trainer on the BBC digital storytelling project, *Capture Wales*, suggestion that the self-representations produced by *Capture Wales*, taken together, problematise representations of Welsh history (as discussed in Chapter 4). And they are clear in the interviews with participants in *London's Voices* discussed in Chapter 5. 'Kimberley' and friends articulated their reason's for participating in *London's Voices 16–19* in terms of the changes that they wanted to see and the democratic voice that they wanted to take up. Moreover the interview revealed a sophisticated familiarity with media discourse about 'people like them' and the ability playfully to critique such a discourse via the activity of self-representation. Thus 'Kimberley' claims 'ordinariness' for her family and friends against hyperbolic, racialised media representations of racial difference:

> **'Kimberley':** This is 'the difference between black and white'. [Pointing to a photograph of two boys – one black and one white – sitting on a wall with graffiti in the background,] Laughs.
> **Interviewer:** What is the difference?
> **'Kimberley:** I'm joking, that's my brother. And then there's the graffiti.

Here 'Kimberley' plays with me, the interviewer. Describing one of her own photographs, she employs the kind of slogan typically found in mainstream media representations: 'the difference between black and white'. When asked to elaborate, 'Kimberley' shows that she had me fooled: 'I'm joking'. Finally, she powerfully undercuts the kind of labelling she has referred to by humanising the people in the photograph and in so doing challenges this kind of media discourse and, by extension, anyone who might take it seriously.

Supporting the history of work in audience studies, people who make and display their own self-representations know, just as the producers know, that 'ordinary people' carries negative, denigratory connotations and they play with those when they can.

The discussion of self-representation in reality TV, in Chapter 4, showed how institutional legitimacy rests on other kinds of value to those in the museum, arts and public service broadcasting discussed above. In reality TV particular kinds of self-representation are repeated so that what emerges is not a diversification of representation or a challenge to stereotypical representation, but rather precisely the opposite. Thus we have seen how self-representation in reality TV constructs the denigratory meaning of the 'ordinary person' although, clearly, processes of mediation render this picture complicated; the processes of textual mediation are contradictory for we sympathise with Mick's predicament in Channel Four's *Faking It* and laugh with him at the pretentiousness of the London fashion world, while at the same time being invited to be entertained by the incongruity of this factory worker from the north of England existing in this setting. Meanwhile the processes of institutional and cultural mediation also require picking apart. While interviewing viewers of reality TV for the Economic and Social Research Council Making Class and Self Through Televised Ethical Scenarios (ESRC) project on reality TV audiences, I was told by one respondent about her experience of being used regularly as a contributor to TV particularly when producers were searching for people to talk about the experience of teen pregnancy.[3] This young woman gave an account of how heavily the producers relied on her and her reluctance to oblige on occasions when her priority was to spend time with her children instead. I would not argue that this young woman had the power to represent herself as she pleases nor that she achieves economic value via this exchange, but only note that this anecdote highlights the woman's agency in this exchange and suggest that such a dynamic contributes to the processes of mediation at hand.

The discussion of inadvertent and banal self-representation online in Chapter 6 cements the importance of close analysis of mediation processes in institutional, textual and cultural dimensions by drawing attention to the centrality of self-representation to, for example, a social networking site such as Facebook in which socialising is the stated aim but in which self-representation is always a condition of participation. Attention to the role of mediation processes in shaping self-representation in such a context highlights how claims made by the institutions enabling self-representation (in this example, the commercial company, Facebook) are always political and always take place within the broader context of digital culture in which there are inequalities around literacy (including, still, access) and representation. Thus to return to Mouffe's definition of 'politics' and the 'political' which was discussed in Chapter 1, when textual self-representations are produced as an everyday part of socialising online, itself an everyday activity for many people across the world now, the question is raised as to the implications of such representation for both 'politics' and the 'political'. How does representing oneself in the service of socialising online relate to democratic representation (if it does at all) and how does representing oneself in the service of socialising contribute to debates about the state of representation of particular individuals and groups in society?

As research has long made clear (see, for example, Coleman, 1997; Corner, 1994; Couldry, 2000a; Livingstone and Lunt, 1994), people who represent themselves in *any* of the settings examined in the preceding pages are doing so from a structurally different power position from those people, and institutions, and companies which facilitate the participation through a workshop or through providing the setting or through producing the programme. However the question of who these self-representing ordinary people are and how they came to be making their self representations is also revealing of the differences between the various examples of the genre of self-representation. Thus we have encountered, for example, self-representations by community group members, journalists, members of black and ethnic minority groups, members of the white working class, actors playing 'ordinary people', people gathered together because they are resident in an area of Bristol or an area of Wales, elderly people with memories of South London or memories of the depression era in the USA, users of Facebook. All of this variety breaks up the idea of *the* ordinary person and yet, paradoxically, each example serves to connote 'ordinary' and construct the genre of self-representation.

The connotations of the construction 'community' were discussed in Chapter 2. The idea that 'community' operates as a claim, as a desire, as well as symbolically, has been noted by scholars (Anderson, 1991; Silverstone, 1999). Moreover, it was suggested that 'community' summons an image of people, not institutions (Williams, 1983), but that the concept, because of its symbolic connotation, is dangerous, because in invoking some people it excludes others (Bauman, 2001; Hall, 1999). Rose's reference to the influence of American Liberal Communitarian thinkers like Etzioni (1997) and Putnam (2000) on British New Labour's Third Way was noted, as was Mayo's suggestion that 'community' *is itself* currently functioning *as* policy.

Rose and Mayo have both suggested that the idea of 'community' has become a key concept in contemporary policy and politics (Mayo, 2006; Rose, 2001):

> The communitarian answer to the crisis of values, however, differs from that proposed by neoconservatives. What was necessary was not strong government but the recreation of civic engagement. Moral order cannot rest on legal codes enforced and upheld by guardians; it is embodied and taught through the rituals and traditions in the everyday life of 'communities'. Hence a strategy to recreate civic morality cannot succeed if it seeks to articulate and enforce a fixed set of virtues, but must seek to recreate 'community' engagement, to foster moral dialogue within and among diverse 'communities' around a minimum set of core values shared by all.
>
> (Rose, 2001, p. 7)

Rose is here talking about neo-liberalism, but recent scholarship discussing conservative policy also suggests advances in the same project:

> My argument is that the present situation is a crisis, another unresolved rupture of that conjuncture which we can define as 'the long march of the Neoliberal Revolution'. Each crisis since the 1970s has looked different, arising from specific historical circumstances. However, they also seem to share some consistent underlying features, to be connected in their general thrust and direction of travel. Paradoxically, opposed political regimes have all contributed in different ways to expanding this project
>
> (Hall, 2011, pp. 9–10)

In terms of the particular focus on community, Mayo noted the risks, but also the benefits, to members of the public of what she described as 'community as policy'. Throughout the examples discussed in preceding chapters I suggest that some notion of 'community' repeatedly emerges as important to the mediation of self-representations. The ubiquity of the construct 'community' in the discourse surrounding *diverse self-representations* adds support to Rose's claim that the concept can be understood as a tool of governance. Furthermore, the ubiquity of 'community' in the producer discourse, in particular, suggests that 'community' *is* policy, not only in the areas of regeneration and development on which Mayo focuses, but also in the digital culture more generally.

An exploration of processes of mediation allows us to see behind-the-scenes of the discourse to which Rose refers. While the term 'community' is ubiquitous, at the same time, there is considerable tension over what it means. 'Community' is both the place where the audience is located and an ideal that self-representation should contribute to bringing into being. Producers' use of the term 'community' seems to signal the desire to unite people, across their differences (whether to produce profit or to enable a 'democratic voice'). Silverstone's observations, that 'community' always operates as a claim and that believing in community brings it into being, are both supported by the examples discussed in preceding chapters. This was very clear in the observation of group events – the workshops run by *Capture Wales*, the young people taking photographs for *16–19*, and even the 'community' created by the juxtaposition of individual and group experience on the websites of *London's Voices* and *Capture Wales*. It is also clear in the commonsensical notion of a 'community' of Facebook or YouTube users.

The investigation of the processes of institutional mediation shows that 'communities' are sometimes built across difference, for example, in the bringing together of people who would never normally meet, such as in the *Capture Wales* workshop. At the same time the detailed exploration of the processes of production highlighted that, in giving voice to distinct 'communities', it is shown to be challenging to try to unite them across their difference. In both *London's Voices* and *Capture Wales*, analyses of the processes of textual mediation showed that 'community' was built in the presentation of diverse individual stories on the websites as much, if not more, than among the people themselves in their material lives. Moreover, contradictory definitions of 'community' emerge from the analyses of diverse examples of self-representations: 'community' as singular, plural, existing and lacking as a positive and as a negative and as an innocent ascription, as national, international and transnational. Public service institutions continue in their longstanding role of assisting in the imagination of a national 'community' (Alexander and Jacobs, 1998; Anderson, 1991; Silverstone, 1999). However, at least on the part of the institutions making these projects, imagining national 'community' is today about imagining, constituting and giving space to the diverse 'communities' that make up the nation, supporting much recent academic work which suggests that, as Silverstone puts it, the casualty is the national 'community' (Silverstone, 1999).

This study finds categorical support for Livingstone and Lunt's earlier suggestion with regards to audience participation in talk shows that the opportunity to speak comes with limits (Livingstone and Lunt, 1994). The self-representations we have looked at speak from personal and experiential perspectives – this is what self-representation has come to mean. Before we immediately assume that speaking from personal perspectives is a drawback or a weakness, however, we must recall the dimension of cultural mediation. We have seen that people *enjoy* speaking from experience and, in fact, *expect* the opportunity to speak from experience as an intrinsic part of the process of producing their own self-representation. In some cases, people took part in a project inviting self-representation precisely because the process afforded them the opportunity to speak – and think – about personal experience. 'Rebecca' and 'Vikram', for example, were two participants in *Capture Wales* who found it valuable to think about their lives. 'Vikram' found himself delving into family history in a way that he had not done before and in a way that he hoped might have wider, political, ramifications; he hoped that the audience he imagined *for* his self-representation might reconsider their attitudes to refugees. Some teenage participants in the *London's Voices 16–19* project expected that speaking from their experience might have led to improvements to their physical environment.

These examples show that the process of 'speaking from experience' can have a range of benefits. Sometimes these benefits are private, as was the case when I was reprimanded by a participant in *Capture Wales* for asking the wrong questions when I asked the focus group participants why the BBC was doing this kind of project. This participant said that I should rather ask what people get out of participating. In some cases, speaking from experience served less private intentions, as in the examples of 'Vikram', the refugee from Fiji, discussed above or the young people who participated in *London's Voices 16–19*, or the black and minority ethnic participants in *London's*

Voices. All of these participants hoped that speaking from experience would impact upon how they were perceived and understood by the wider public.

Now, this view of the value of speaking from experience connects to wider debates about the public sphere. This value placed on personal experience in public recalls Van Zoonen's argument that the visibility of 'humdrum experience' in public is valuable because it changes the bounds of what is an acceptable part of public discourse (Van Zoonen, 2001). And, at the same time, the value placed on personal experience, as potentially leading to change, recalls ideas about the relation between how what takes place in media spaces does or does not lead to actual material change beyond media spaces – an issue raised, for example, by Fenton (2007).

That people who make self-representations tend to do so from a personal and experiential perspective suggests that audiences who participate are fixed in place as 'ordinary people', as the bearers of experience and, as such, are different from the inhabitants of media worlds, recalling Couldry's division between media and ordinary worlds (Couldry, 2000a). Private subject matter is associated with the genre of self-representation and the constructions of 'ordinary people' speaking from, and/or located in, 'communities'. Finally, private subject matter is associated with texts that are identifiably that of the genre of self-representation, bearing the 'quality' of the amateur aesthetic. Now, this 'amateur aesthetic' can be read as positive – the claiming of a distinct aesthetic (in Atton's terms) – but it can also be seen as resulting in a fixing in place (in Bourdieu's terms), as precisely *not* being equivalent to the consecrated arts of fine artists and film-makers, who operate in public as professionals (Atton, 2002; Bourdieu, 1990 (1965)). Of course, the engagement of professional artists and documentary film-makers in this terrain complicates the picture, their work also contributing to a challenging of the boundaries between amateur and professional and perhaps indicating changes to come (Dovey and Rose, forthcoming).

While the self-representations explored in this study contribute to a widening of what is deemed worthy of public exhibition, at the same time the question is raised as to the implications beyond representation, of this change in public subject matter. Livingstone suggests,

The resources, the competences, the motivations which lead people to participate in public draw – in a manner little understood – on the lived experiences and activities, the conditions and constraints, the identities and relationships of people in their status as private individuals. In other words, rather than denigrating certain kinds of sociality as 'less than public' – as pre- or proto- or quasi-public – we could ask, what does it take for people to participate in public, what does the public require, what are its preconditions?

(Livingstone, 2005b, pp. 28–9)

Tracing the link between self-representation and material political action is beyond the scope of this book, but it is clear that the question of how self-representations are mediated is absolutely a key precursor to any such investigation. In his earlier discussion of Access TV, Corner noted,

For it is how 'ordinary people' appear and speak on television, within particular formats, which determines both the character and the success of 'access' socially and politically.

(1994, p. 20)

Analysis of mediation processes highlights political difference between examples of self-representation that may look alike. But we have to return to the idea of the genre of self-representations to see that people are fixed, at least in the moment of the self-representation. The notion of some kind of mediated public space is necessary for thinking about what happens when audiences come into contact with the media and, in particular, when they make representations of themselves to be disseminated publicly. We can call on the idea of a mediated public space without upholding Habermas' ideal type public sphere, as Livingstone notes,

After all, the media are not so successful in managing their complex institutions, texts and audiences so as to exclude deliberation, contestation, even transgression. Perhaps the media can, under certain conditions, play a role in exploring or challenging the limits of governmentality rather than merely serving as the instrument of its ever-more efficient control. Where else, after all, could such contestation occur if not in mediated spaces?

(Livingstone, 2005b, pp. 36–7)

We might consider the operation of the notion of *'community'* and the construct of the *'ordinary person'* as governing structures through a metaphor of cracks and valves in structures. We might imagine valves in the structures of governance, whereby self-representation in mediated public spaces does nothing more than maintain the status quo – because it *allows* people to speak for themselves as a way of pacifying any demands to actually be heard through meaningful democratic representation. Note the London youth worker's remarks that the young people he works with are accustomed to being asked what they think, but just not yet to seeing anything happen as a result of what they say, or the 'liking' of the declaration 'Get the Fascist BNP off Facebook' as the limit of political action. Alternatively, we might imagine cracks in structures, whereby there is a breaking through or a breaking down of the status quo through an undermining of what 'community' is about and what 'ordinary people' means. For it is clear that varied examples of self-representation never remove tensions in what 'community' membership means. On the contrary, since self-representation very often involves collaboration or co-production, the ways in which individual participants position themselves – as *'ordinary'*, as belonging to a *'community'*, or not – cannot be, and the empirical work suggests are not, fully controlled in any setting. It follows that what 'community' and 'ordinary' *mean*, and therefore how they function, is also beyond complete control. It is in fact the site of power struggle – a struggle that becomes clear through the empirical exploration of how the processes of mediation shape the genre of self-representation.

Notes

1 Introduction: Self-Representation and Digital Culture

1. The Community Programme Unit was established by the BBC in the early 1970s as part of the Access movement in UK broadcasting. See, for example, Corner (1994). *Mass Observation* was a 1930s project which documented 'ordinary' life through the use of observers and diarists. See, for example, Highmore (2002).
2. Illouz focuses her discussion on the USA but the argument can be extended from American society to the West in general.
3. Contemporary institutional discourses of participatory community are part of what has been called the Post-Washington consensus wherein policies of the New Right were followed by attempts by the Clinton and Blair administrations to temper the free reign of the market in some areas of life (see Mayo, 2006).
4. See the highly publicised invitation in 2010 to the public in the UK to contribute to a British Museum/BBC project called *A History of the World in 100 Objects*: 'Add your object and help tell a history of our world' – http://www.bbc.co.uk/ahistoryoftheworld/about/. Instructions stated that the personal should link to broader historical processes – so that ordinary experience is used to shed light on known historical events.
5. *London's Voices* was a Heritage Lottery funded project at the Museum of London from 2001 to 2004, run jointly by the Oral History & Contemporary Collecting and the Access and Learning Departments. *Capture Wales* was a BBC Wales digital storytelling project initiated by BBC Wales and the Cardiff School of Journalism, Media and Cultural Studies at Cardiff University. The project was funded by the BBC and ran from 2001 to 2008 (with initial funding for three years) (http://www.bbc.co.uk/wales/arts/yourvideo/about.shtml). *Capture Wales* was modelled on the practice and definition of digital storytelling developed by Joe Lambert and colleagues at The Center for Digital Storytelling in the San Francisco Bay Area, California, established in the 1990s (http://www.storycenter.org/history.html). See also Lambert (2006), which has subsequently been adopted and adapted across the world (see Hartley and McWilliam, 2009).
6. Earlier formulations of some of the ideas presented in this book have been published or presented (see Enli and Thumim, 2009; Thumim, 2008, 2009a, 2009b, 2010).
7. *Faking It*, Channel Four, First Broadcast 19 September 2004.

3 Mediation

1. See the Mediatized Stories Network. Mediatized Stories: Mediation Perspectives among Youth. http://www.uv.uio.no/intermedia/english/research/projects/mediatized-stories/.

2. Understanding a Local Media Ecology Research Project 2011–12, Institute of Communication Studies, University of Leeds, research team: Professor Stephen Coleman, Professor Jay G. Blumler, Judith Stamper, Dr Giles Moss, Dr Nancy Thumim, Stephen McDermott.
3. The Culture Vulture: http://theculturevulture.co.uk/blog/.
4. Mike Chitty: http://oursociety.org.uk/profile/MikeChitty.
5. See Livingstone (2005b) for a discussion of the history of the concepts 'audience' and 'public' and their very different connotations.

4 Broadcasters

1. See Wardle and Williams (2008) on this range just within the BBC.
2. January–April 2004 was spent conducting the qualitative research on *Capture Wales*. This included interviews with participants and producers, observations of workshops, and documentary analysis. A further interview was carried out in March 2005, with Daniel Meadows, Creative Director of *Capture Wales*.
3. For discussions of the politics of reality TV across the world see, for example, Kraidy and Sender (2011).
4. Making Class and Self through Televised Ethical Scenarios April 2005–September 2007: (ESRC 148-25-0040); grant holder, Bev Skeggs; co-applicant, Helen Wood; researcher, Nancy Thumim (October 2005–April 2007).
5. Retrieved 29 June 2005 from: http://www.bbc.co.uk/wales/capturewales/about/.
6. Retrieved 4 July 2005 from: http://www.bbc.co.uk/wales/capturewales/background/dai-evans.shtml.
7. The Center for Digital Storytelling website explains:

> In the early 1990s, a group of media artists, designers and practitioners came together in the San Francisco Bay Area, California to explore how personal narrative and storytelling could inform the emergence of a new set of digital media tools. The Center for Digital Storytelling partnership grew out of the numerous collaborations and shared dialogues that occurred during this period. http://www.storycenter.org/history.html.
>
> (See also Lambert, 2006)

8. For a further discussion of digital storytelling as practiced at BBC Wales, see Meadows (2003).
9. *Faking It*, Channel Four, first broadcast 19 September 2004.
10. For quite a different use of the digital storytelling form, see Beeson and Miskelly's work on the use of digital storytelling processes to tell a communal 'story', rather than to bring together individual stories (Beeson and Miskelly, 2005).
11. Gilly Adams at the Digital Storytelling Conference, Cardiff, 2003. Notes from the conference.

12. Notes from the Digital Storytelling Conference, Cardiff, 2003.
13. Ibid. Interviews with members of the *Capture Wales* production team.
14. For example: Interviews with Maggie Russell, Head of Talent, BBC Wales; Daniel Meadows, Creative Director, *Capture Wales*; Gilly Adams, Head of Writers' Unit, BBC Wales, and leader of the Capture Wales Story Circle.
15. Notes from the Digital Storytelling Conference, Cardiff, 2003.
16. The *Capture Wales* project led to two sister projects in two BBC English regions, Lancashire and Humber. These were modelled on the *Capture Wales* form but did not last as long – the *Telling Lives* projects ended in 2005.
17. The *Where I Live* sites host local news and information to which members of the public can contribute, as well as hosting *Video Nation*, in common with many other *Where I Live* sites across the UK. The community studios are places where members of the public can learn media skills and find out about and 'engage with' the BBC. (Interview with Mandy Rose, Editor, New Media, BBC Wales.)
18. Pat Loughrey, Director, BBC Nations and Regions. Notes from the Digital Storytelling Conference, Cardiff, 2003.
19. Notes from the Digital Storytelling Conference, Cardiff, 2003.
20. Emma Trollope, Audience Research, BBC Wales. Notes from a phone call.
21. Interview with David Cartwright, Head of Press and Publicity, BBC Wales.
22. Sparkler Report (2004), internal report about BBC user-generated projects. Press articles copied and collected by David Cartwright, Head of Press and Publicity, BBC Wales.
23. Interview with Daniel Meadows, Creative Director, *Capture Wales*.

5   Museums and Art Worlds

1. September–December 2003 was spent conducting the majority of the qualitative research on *London's Voices*. This included interviews with participants, museum staff, funders and associated bodies; observations of workshops and meetings; and documentary analysis. Additional interviews and observations took place on occasions throughout 2004.
2. Notes from Oral History Society Annual Conference, 2004.
3. Ibid.
4. Ibid.
5. Interview with Annette Day, Curator, Oral History and Contemporary Collecting, Museum of London.
6. Notes from Oral History Society Annual Conference, 2004.
7. Interview with Frazer Swift, Deputy Head of Access and Learning/Project Manager, *London's Voices*.
8. *London's Voices* was a three-year project of activities and exhibitions at the Museum of London from March 2001 to June 2004, funded by the Heritage Lottery Fund (HLF).
9. Interview with Frazer Swift, Deputy Head of Department, Access and Learning/Project Manager, *London's Voices*.

10. The following excerpts are from the Smithsonian Institute's *Strategic Plan* (accessed September 2009) taken from the Smithsonian Institute website (comprising a number of museums and including the Smithsonian Museum).
11. Heritage Lottery Fund.
12. Smithsonian *About 2009*. http://americanart.si.edu/visit/about/retrieved 24 September 2009.
13. Smithsonian *1930s Family Day*. Advisory pdf downloaded from http://americanart.si.edu/pr retrieved 1 May 2009.
14. See, for example, Leo Marx's classic discussion of the 'technological sublime' in nineteenth-century American Literature (Marx, 1964).
15. See, for example, the Knowle West Media Centre Conference, *Socially Engaged Arts Practice in a Changing Political Climate*, September 2010. At this two-day event was attended by artists, community activists and workers, members of the public, arts policy professionals, representatives of national arts institutions and academics, at whom the label 'Socially Engaged Arts Practice' was directed in a number of ways including to describe art work which aimed to engage a wide audience in its reception as well as art work which included members of the public in its conception and/or production.
16. http://www.kwmc.org.uk/index.php?article=387 retrieved 18 October 2010.
17. http://www.arnolfini.org.uk/whatson/events/details/466 retrieved 10 November 2009.
18. http://www.arnolfini.org.uk/pages/about/ retrieved 18 October 2010.
19. http://www.knowlewest.co.uk/2010/05/university-of-local-knowledge-ulk-wiki-sessions/ retrieved 18 October 2010.
20. Of course the question of technological properties and democratic praxis leads to a wider area of debate about the role (and challenges) of new media in organising for social change. See, for example, Fenton (2007).
21. www.museumoflondon.org.uk/ retrieved 29 June 2005.
22. www.museumoflondon.org.uk/MOLsite/londonsvoices/ retrieved 5 July 2003.
23. Ibid.
24. Ibid.
25. Ibid.

6   Self-Representation Online

1. With thanks to Professor Stephen Coleman for suggesting this formulation on reading an earlier draft of this chapter.
2. We must note the economic and political environment of recession that forms the context to these changes as discussed in Chapter 4. This context is currently having an impact on cultural policy across the world – in this particular case, there is a 25% cut to the BBC online budget (Hunter, 2011).
3. http://www.facebook.com/group.php?gid=2517126532 retrieved 12 September 2011.

4. Meadows is articulating here the ethos of a longstanding tradition of community arts practice.
5. http://www.facebook.com/facebookAbout retrieved 11 September 2011.
6. http://www.storycenter.org/principles.html retrieved 8 July 2011.

7 Self-Representation, Digital Culture and Genre

1. For example, see the widespread use of the services of the Center for Digital Storytelling in Berkeley, California: 'The majority of our work is carried out in close partnership with a wide range of community, educational, health and human services, international development and business organizations, in the form of Customized Program Development for digital storytelling. This approach allows us to draw upon our expertise as pioneers in the field, as we work closely with clients to identify and meet specific needs in unique contexts around the world.' (Center for Digital Storytelling, Our Services)
2. See Carpentier (2007), for a discussion of different degrees of public participation in media institutions.
3. Making Class and Self through Televised Ethical Scenarios April 2005–September 2007: (ESRC 148-25-0040), grant holder, Bev Skeggs; co-applicant, Helen Wood; researcher, Nancy Thumim (October 2005–April 2007).

Bibliography

Abercrombie, N. and Longhurst, B. (1998) *Audiences: A Sociological Theory of Performance and Imagination* (London: Sage Publications).

Adorno, T. and Horkheimer, M. (Eds) (1993 [1944]) 'The Culture Industry: Enlightenment as Mass Deception', *Dialectic of Enlightenment* (New York: Continuum).

Alexander, J. C. and Jacobs, R. N. (1998) 'Mass Communication, Ritual and Civil Society', in J. Curran and T. Liebes (Eds) *Media, Ritual and Identity* (London: Routledge).

Altman, R. (1999) *Film Genre* (London: BFI Palgrave Macmillan).

Anderson, B. (1991 [1983]) *Imagined Communities: Reflections on the Origin and Spread of Nationalism* (London: Verso).

Andrejevic, M. (2004) *Reality TV: The Work of Being Watched* (Lanham, MD: Rowman & Littlefield Publishers).

Ang, I. (1990) *Desperately Seeking the Audience* (London and New York: Routledge).

Arts Council of England, http://www.artscouncil.org.uk/aboutus/agenda.php, retrieved 10 July 2008.

Asthma UK Get It Off Your Chest website, http://getitoffyourchest.asthma. org.uk/, retrieved 8 August 2011.

Atton, C. (2002) *Alternative Media* (London: Sage Publications).

Bakardjieva, M. (2005) *Internet Society: The Internet in Everyday Life* (London and Thousand Oaks, CA, and New Delhi: Sage Publications).

Barthes, R. (1973 [1957]) *Mythologies* (London: Paladin).

Bauman, Z. (2001) *Community: Seeking Safety in an Insecure World* (Cambridge: Polity Press).

BBC (2011) 'About the BBC Blog', http://www.bbc.co.uk/blogs/aboutthebbc/ 2011/01/delivering-quality-first.shtml, retrieved 17 February 2011.

BBC (2010) *Strategy Review*, March, http://downloads.bbc.co.uk/aboutthebbc/ reports/pdf/strategy_review.pdf, retrieved 18 May 2011.

BBC (2004) *Building Public Value: Renewing the BBC for a Digital World* (London: BBC).

BBC (2003) 'BBC Wales Annual Review 2002–2003', http://www.bbc.co.uk/ wales/info/review_2003/connecting_communities.shtml, retrieved 6 June 2004.

BBC Committees of Enquiry, bbc.co.uk/heritage/resources/pdfs/committees_ of_enquiry.pdf, retrieved 27 February 2006.

Beck, U. (1992) *The Risk Society: Towards a New Modernity* (London: Sage Publications).

Beeson, I. and Miskelly, C. (2005) 'Digital Stories of Community: Mobilization, Coherence & Continuity', paper presented at *Media in Transition 4: The Work of Stories* (Cambridge, MA: MIT).

Bennett, T. (2006) 'Exhibition, Difference, and the Logic of Culture', in I. Karp et al (Eds) *Museum Frictions Public Cultures/Global Transformations* (Durham and London: Duke University Press).

Bennett, T. (1995) *The Birth of the Museum: History, Theory, Politics* (London: Routledge).

Berger, J. (1967) 'The Moment of Cubism', *New Left Review*, 42 (March–April), 75–94.

Bergeron, S. (2003) 'The Post-Washington Consensus and Economic Representations of Women in Development at the World Bank', *International Feminist Journal of Politics*, 5(3), 397–419.

Billig, M. (1999) 'Whose Terms? Whose Ordinariness? Rhetoric and Ideology in Conversation Analysis', *Discourse & Society*, 10, 543–58.

Billig, M (1995) *Banal Nationalism* (London: Sage Publications).

Bolin, G. (2010) 'Digitization, Multiplatform Texts, and Audience Reception', *Popular Communication*, 8(1), 72–83.

Bolter, J. D. and Grusin, R. (1999) *Remediation: Understanding New Media* (Cambridge: MIT Press).

Bonner, F. (2003) *Ordinary Television* (London and Thousand Oaks, CA and New Delhi: Sage Publications).

Born, G. (2004) *Uncertain Vision: Birt, Dyke and the Reinvention of the BBC* (London: Secker and Warburg).

Boswell, D. and Evans, J. (Eds.) (1999) *Representing the Nation: A Reader. Histories, Heritage and Museums* (London and New York: Routledge in association with the Open University).

Bourdieu, P. (1990 [1965]) *Photography: A Middle-brow Art* (S. Whiteside, Trans.) (Stanford: Stanford University Press).

boyd, d. (2006) 'Friends, Friendsters and MySpace Top 8: Writing Community into Being on Social Network Sites.' *First Monday* 11:12, December. http://www.firstmonday.org/issues/issue11_12/boyd/index.html

Boyd-Barrett, O. and Newbold, C. (1995) 'Editors' Introduction: Approaching the Field', in O. Boyd-Barrett and C. Newbold (Eds) *Approaches to Media: A Reader* (London: Arnold).

BP website, http://www.bp.com/sectiongenericarticle.do?categoryId=9036379&contentId=7067216, retrieved 8 July 2011.

Buckingham, D. (2010) 'Do We Really Need Media Education 2.0? Teaching in the Age of Participatory Media', in K. Drotner and K. C. Schroeder (Eds) *Digital Content Creation: Perceptions, Practices and Perspectives* (Oxford: Peter Lang).

Buckingham, D. (2009) ' "Creative" Visual Methods in Media Research: Possibilities, Problems and Proposals', *Media, Culture and Society*, 31(4), 633–52.

Buckingham, D. (2007) *Beyond Technology: Children's Learning in the Age of Digital Culture* (Cambridge: Polity Press).

Buckingham, D. (1987) *Public Secrets: EastEnders and Its Audience* (London: BFI).

Burgess, J. (2006) 'Hearing Ordinary Voices. Continuum', *Journal of Media & Culture* 20(2), 201–14.

Burgess, J. and Green, J. (2009) *YouTube*, Digital Media and Society Series (Cambridge: Polity).

Burgess J. E. and Klaebe H. G. (2009) 'Digital Storytelling as Participatory Public History in Australia', in J. Hartley and K. McWilliam (Eds.) *Story Circle: Digital Storytelling Around the World* (Oxford: Wiley-Blackwell) 155–66.

Burn, A. and Parker, D. (2003) *Analysing Media Texts* (London and New York: Continuum).

Butler, J. (1990) *Gender Trouble: Feminism and the Subversion of Identity* (London: Routledge).

Cammaerts, B. (2007) 'Media and Communication Strategies of Glocalized Activists: Beyond Media-Centric Thinking', in B. Cammaerts and N. Carpentier (Eds) *Reclaiming the Media: Communication Rights and Democratic Media Roles* (Bristol and Chicago: Intellect Books).

Carey, J. (1992) *Communication as Culture: Essays on Media and Society* (London: Routledge).

Carpentier, N. (2011) *Media and Participation: A Site of Ideological-Democratic Struggle* (Bristol: Intellect).

Carpentier, N. (2007) 'Coping with the Agoraphobic Media Professional: A Typology of Journalistic Practices Reinforcing Democracy and Participation', in B. Cammaerts and N. Carpentier (Eds) *Reclaiming the Media: Communication Rights and Democratic Media Roles*, (Bristol and Chicago: Intellect Books) 157–75.

Carpentier, N. and Hannot, W. (2009) 'To Be a Common Hero: The Uneasy Balance between the Ordinary and Ordinariness in the Subject Position of Mediated Ordinary People in the Talk Show Jan Publiek', *International Journal of Cultural Studies*, 12(6), 597–616.

Castells, M. (2001) *The Internet Galaxy, Reflections on the Internet, Business and Society* (Oxford: Oxford University Press).

Center For Digital Storytelling, http://www.storycenter.org/index1.html, retrieved 15 July 2011.

Chandler, D (1997) 'An Introduction to Genre Theory', http://www.aber.ac.uk/media/Documents/intgenre/chandler_genre_theory.pdf, retrieved 17 May 2011.

Cheung, C. (2000) 'A Home on the Web: Presentations of Self on Personal Homepages', in D. Gauntlett (Ed.) *Web Studies: Rewiring Media Studies for the Digital Age* (London: Arnold).

Chouliaraki, L. (2006) 'Towards an Analytics of Mediation', *Critical Discourse Studies*, 3(2), 153–78.

Christensen, C. L. (2010) 'Lifestyle as Factual Entertainment', in J. Gripsrud (Ed.) *Relocating Television: Television in the Digital Context* (Routledge: London).

Code, L (1993) 'Taking Subjectivity into Account', in L. Alcoff and L. Potter (Eds) *Feminist Epistemologies* (Oxon: Routledge).

Coleman, E. G. (2010) 'Ethnographic Approaches to Digital Media', *Annual Review of Anthropology*, 39, 487–505.

Coleman, S. (forthcoming) 'The Internet and the Opening Up of Political Space', in J. Hartley, J. Burgess and A. Bruns (Eds) *Blackwell Companion to New Media Dynamics* (Malden, MA: Wiley-Blackwell).

Coleman, S. (2006) 'How the Other Half Votes: Big Brother Viewers and the 2005 British General Election Campaign', *International Journal of Cultural Studies*, 9(4), 457–80.

Coleman, S. (1997) *Stilled Tongues: From Soapbox to Soundbite* (London: Porcupine Press).

Coleman, S. and Blumler J. G. (2009) *The Internet and Democratic Citizenship: Theory, Practice and Policy* (Cambridge: Cambridge University Press).

Coleman, S. and Ross, K. (2010) *The Media and the Public: Them and Us in Media Discourse* (Oxford: Blackwell Publishers).

Corner, J. (2010) ' "Critical Social Optics" and the Transformations of Audio-Visual Culture', in J. Gripsrud (Ed.) *Relocating Television: Television in the Digital Context* (London: Routledge).

Corner, J. (2009) 'Public Knowledge and Popular Culture: Spaces and Tensions', *Media, Culture and Society*, 31(1), 141–9.

Corner, J. (1999) *Critical Ideas in Television Studies* (Oxford: Oxford University Press).

Corner, J. (1995a) *Television Form and Public Address* (London: Edward Arnold).

Corner, J. (1995b) 'Media Studies and the "Knowledge Problem" ', *Screen*, 36(2), 147–55.

Corner, J. (1994) 'Mediating the Ordinary: The "Access" Idea and Television Form', in M. Aldridge and N. Hewitt (Eds.) *Controlling Broadcasting: Access Policy and Practice in North America and Europe* (Manchester: Manchester University Press).

Corner, J. (1991) 'Meaning, Genre and Context: The Problematics of "Public Knowledge", in the New Audience Studies', in J. Curran and M. Gurevitch (Eds) *Mass Media and Society* (London: Edward Arnold).

Corner, J. and Harvey, S. (Eds) (1991) *Enterprise and Heritage: Crosscurrents of National Culture* (London and New York: Routledge).

Corner, J., Harvey, S. and Lury, K. (1994) 'Culture, Quality and Choice: The Re-Regulation of TV 1989–91', in S. Hood (Ed.) *Behind the Screens: The Structure of British Broadcasting in the Nineties* (London: Lawrence and Wishart).

Corner, J., Richardson, K. and Fenton, N. (1990) *Nuclear Reactions: Form and Response in Public Issue Television* (London: John Libbey & Company Ltd).

Couldry, N. (2010) *Why Voice Matters: Culture and Politics After Neoliberalism* (London: Sage Publications).

Couldry, N. (2008) 'Mediatization or Mediation? Alternative Understandings of the Emergent Space of Digital Storytelling', *New Media & Society*, 10(3), 373–91.

Couldry, N. (2006) *Listening Beyond the Echoes: Media, Ethics and Agency in an Uncertain World* (Boulder, CO: Paradigm Publishers).

Couldry, N. (2004) 'Theorizing Media as Practice', *Social Semiotics*, 14(2), 115–32.

Couldry, N. (2002) 'Playing for Celebrity: "Big Brother as Ritual Event"', *Television and New Media*, 3(3), 283–93.

Couldry, N. (2000a) *The Place of Media Power: Pilgrims and Witnesses of the Media Age* (London: Routledge).

Couldry, N. (2000b) *Inside Culture: Re-Imagining the Method of Cultural Studies* (London: Sage Publications).

D'Acci, J. (1994) *Defining Women: Television and the Case of Cagney and Lacey* (London: University of North Carolina Press).

Dahlberg, L. (2001) 'Democracy via Cyberspace: Mapping the Rhetorics and Practices of Three Prominent Camps', *New Media and Society*, 13(2), 157–77.

Davison, S., Hall, S., Rustin, M. and Rutherford, J. (2010) ' "Labour in a Time of Coalition" A Roundtable Discussion of What the Future Holds for Labour' (Soundings and Open Left) 21 May, http://www.lwbooks.co.uk/journals/soundings/articles/s45Coalition.pdf, retrieved 27 October 2011.

DCMS (2005) *Understanding the Future: Museums and 21st Century Life* (London: DCMS).

De Tocqueville, A. (1863) *Democracy in America* (H. Reeve, Trans.) (Cambridge: Sever and Francis).

Deuze, M. (2006) 'Participation, Remediation, Bricolage: Considering the Principal Components of a Digital Culture', *The Information Society*, 22, 63–75.

Dovey, J. (2000) *Freakshow: First Person Media and Factual Television* (London: Pluto Press).

Dovey, J. and Lister, M. (2009) 'Straw Men or Cyborgs Interactions', *Studies in Communication and Culture*, 1(1), 129–45.

Dovey, J. and Rose, M. (forthcoming) 'This Great Mapping of Ourselves' – New Documentary Forms Online', in Winston, B. (Ed.) *BFI Companion to Documentary* (London: BFI Publishing).

Eco, U. (1981) *The Role of the Reader: Explorations in the Semiotics of Texts* (London: Hutchinson).

Ellis, J. (2000) *Seeing Things: Television in the Age of Uncertainty* (London: I.B. Tauris Publishers).

Ellis, J. (2010) 'The Digitally Enhanced Audience: New Attitudes to Factual Footage', in J. Gripsrud (Ed.) *Relocating Television: Television in the Digital Context* (London: Routledge).

Ellis, J. (2012) *Documentary: Witness and Self-Revelation* (Oxon: Routledge).

Enli, G. S. and Thumim, N. (2009) 'Socializing and Self-Representation Online: Exploring Facebook', paper presented at *The Presentation of Self in Everyday Digital Life Transforming Audiences 2, Pre-Conference*, 2 September 2009, University of Westminster, London.

Etzioni, A. (1997) *The New Golden Rule: Community and Morality in a Democratic Society* (London: Profile).

Facebook Press Info, https://www.facebook.com/press/info.php?, retrieved 22 August 2011.

Fairclough, N. (1995) *Media Discourse* (Cambridge: Polity).

Fenton, N. (2007) 'Contesting Global Capital New Media, Solidarity, and the Role of the Social Imaginary', in B. Cammaerts and N. Carpentier (Eds) *Reclaiming the Media: Communication Rights and Democratic Media Roles* (Bristol and Chicago: Intellect Books).

Flew, T. and Cunningham, S. (2010) 'Creative Industries after the First Decade of Debate', *The Information Society*, 26(2), 113–23.

Fornäs, J. (2008) 'Bridging Gaps: Ten Crosscurrents in Media Studies', *Media, Culture and Society*, 30(6), 895–905.

Fornäs, J. (2000) 'The Crucial in Between: The Centrality of Mediation in Cultural Studies', *European Journal of Cultural Studies*, 3(1), 43–65.

Fuchs, C. (2011) 'Web 2.0, Prosumption, and Surveillance', *Surveillance & Society*, 8(3), 288–309, http://www.surveillance-and-society.org, Retreived 15 August 2011.

Fuery, K. (2009) *New Media: Culture and Image* (Basingstoke: Palgrave Macmillan).

Gamson, J. (1998) *Freaks Talk Back: Tabloid Talk Shows and Sexual Nonconformity* (Chicago and London: The University of Chicago Press).

Gauntlett, D. (2009) 'Media Studies 2.0: A Response', *Interactions: Studies in Communication and Culture*, 1(1), 147–57.

Gauntlett, D. (2007) 'Media Studies 2.0', http://www.theory.org.uk/mediastudies2.htm, retrieved 15 June 2011.

Gerbner, G. (1995 [1969]) 'Toward "Cultural Indicators": The Analysis of Mass Mediated Public Message Systems', in O. Boyd-Barrett and C. Newbold (Eds) *Approaches to Media: A Reader* (London: Arnold).

Giddens, A. (1991) *Modernity and Self-Identity* (London: Sage Publications).

Gitlin, T. (1998) 'Public Sphere or Public Sphericules?', in J. Curran and T. Liebes (Eds) *Media, Ritual and Identity* (London: Routledge).

Goffman, E. (1959) *Presentation of Self in Everyday Life* (New York: Doubleday and Anchor Books).

Gourd, A. (2002) *Offentlichkeit und digitales Fernsehen*, (Wiesbaden: Westdeutscher Verlag).

Gripsrud, J. (Ed.) (2010a) *Relocating Television: Television in the Digital Context* (London: Routledge).

Gripsrud, J. (2010b) 'Television in the digital public sphere' in Gripsrud, J. (Ed.) *Relocating Television: Television in the Digital Context* (Oxon: Routledge).

Gripsrud, J. (Ed.) (1999) *Television and Common Knowledge* (London: Routledge).

Habermas, J. (1989) *The Structural Transformation of the Public Sphere: An Inquiry into a Category of Bourgeois Society* (T. Burger, Trans.) (Cambridge, MA: MIT Press).

Habermas, J. (1974) 'The Public Sphere: An Encyclopaedia Article', *New German Critique*, 3, 49–55.

Hall, S. (2011) 'The Neoliberal Revolution', *Soundings*, 48 (Summer), 9–27.

Hall, S. (1999) 'Culture, Community, Nation', in D. Boswell and J. Evans (Eds) *Representing the Nation: A Reader. Histories, Heritage and Museums* (London and New York: Routledge).

Hall, S. (Ed.) (1997) *Cultural Representations and Signifying Practices* (London: Open University Press).

Hall, S. (1996) 'Introduction: "Who needs 'Identity'?"', in S. Hall and P. du Gay (Eds.) *Questions of Cultural Identity* (London: Sage Publications).

Hall, S. (1973) 'Encoding and Decoding in the Television Discourse', CCCS Media Series Stencilled Paper No.7. (Birmingham: University of Birmingham Centre for Contemporary Cultural Studies).

Hampton, M. (2001) 'Understanding Media: Theories of the Press in Britain, 1850–1914', *Media, Culture and Society*, 23(2), 213–31.

Hardt, H. (1992) *Crtitical Communication Studies: Communication, History and Theory in America* (London: Routledge).

Hargreaves, I. (2001) *Welsh Lives: A Proposal* (original Capture Wales proposal).

Harrison, J. and Wessels, B. (2005) 'A New Public Service Communication Environment? Public Service Broadcasting Values in the Reconfiguring Media', *New Media and Society*, 17(6), 834–53.

Hartley, J. (2010) 'Where Money and Meanings Meet', in K. Drotner and K. C. Schroeder (Eds) *Digital Content Creation: Perceptions, Practices and Perspectives* (Oxford: Peter Lang).

Hartley, J. (2008) 'Editorial "'Who Are You Going to Believe – Me or Your Own Eyes?' New Decade; New Directions"', *International Journal of Cultural Studies*, 11(1), 5–13.

Hartley, J. (2002) *Communication, Cultural and Media Studies: The Key Concepts* (London: Routledge).

Hartley, J. and McWilliam, K. (Eds) (2009) *Story Circle: Digital Storytelling Around the World* (Oxford: Wiley-Blackwell).

Hein, H. (2000) *The Museum in Transition: A Philosophical Perspective* (Washington, DC: Smithsonian Institution Press).

Held, D. and McGrew, A. (2002) *Globalisation and Anti-Globalisation* (London: Polity Press).

Henning, M. (2006) *Museums, Media and Cultural Theory* (Maidenhead: OU Press).

Heritage Lottery Fund website, http://www.hlf.org.uk/english, retrieved 10 July 2008.

Hermes, J. (2009) 'Audience Studies 2.0. on the Theory, Politics and Method of Qualitative Audience Research', *Interactions: Studies in Communication and Culture* 1(1), 111–28.

Highmore, B. (2002) *Everyday Life and Cultural Theory* (London: Routledge).

Hill, A. (2005) *Reality TV: Audiences and Popular Factual Television* (London: Routledge).

Hill, A. (2002) 'Big Brother: The Real Audience', *Television and New Media*, 3(3), 323–40.

Hill, A., Weibull, L. and Nilsson, A. (2007) 'Public and Popular: British and Swedish Audience Trends in Factual and Reality Television', *Cultural Trends*, 16(1), 17–41.

Hill, A., Palmer, G., Corner, J., Scannell, P., Couldry, N. and Mathijs, E. (2002) 'Big Brother Issue', *Television and New Media*, 3(3), 251–340.

Hoggart, R. (1957) *The Uses of Literacy* (London: Penguin).

Hudson, K. (1999) 'Attempts to Define "Museum" ', in D. Boswell and J. Evans (Eds) *Representing the Nation: A Reader. Histories, Heritage and Museums* (London and New York: Routledge in association with The Open University).

Hunter, I. (2011) 'BBC Internet Blog by Managing Editor BBC Online', http://www.bbc.co.uk/blogs/bbcinternet/2011/01/delivering_quality_first_on_bb.html, retrieved 18 May 2011.

Illouz, E. (2007) *Cold Intimacies: The Making of Emotional Capitalism* (Cambridge: Polity).

Jaworski, A and Bishop, H. (2003) ' "We Beat 'em": Nationalism and the Hegemony of Homogeneity in the British Press Reportage of Germany versus England during Euro 2000', *Discourse & Society*, 14(3), 243–71.

Jenkins, H. (2007) 'Nine Propositions Towards a Cultural Theory of YouTube', http://www.henryjenkins.org/2007/05/9_propositions_towards_a_cultu.html, retrieved 15 October 2007.

Jenkins, H. (2006) *Convergence Culture* (New York: NYU Press).

Karp, I., Kratz, C. A., Szwaja, L., Ybarra-Frausto, T. with Buntinx, G., Kirshenblatt-Gimblett, B. and Rassool, C. (2006) *Museum Frictions: Public Cultures/Global Transformations* (Durham and London: Duke University Press).

Katz, E. (1988) 'Disintermediation: Cutting Out the Middle Man', *Inter Media*, 16(2), 30–1.

Katz, E. and Lazarsfeld, P. F. (1955) *Personal Influence: The Part Played by People in the Flow of Mass Communications* (Glencoe, IL: The Free Press).

Katz, E., Blumler, J. and Gurevitch, M. (Eds) (1974) *The Uses of Mass Communications: Current Perspectives on Gratifications Research* (Beverley Hills: Sage Publications).

Kraidy, M. and Sender, K. (2011) (Eds) *The Politics of Reality Television: Global Perspectives* (London and New York: Routledge).

Kratz, C. A. and Karp, I. (2006) 'Introduction: Museum Frictions: Public Cultures/Global Transformations', in I. Karp, C. A. Kratz, L. Szwaja, T. Ybarra-Frausto, G. Buntinx, B. Kirshenblatt-Gimblett and C. Rassool (Eds) *Museum Frictions: Public Cultures/Global Transformations* (Durham and London: Duke University Press), 1–31.

Lambert, J. (2006) *Digital Storytelling: Capturing Lives, Creating Community*, 2nd edn. (Berkeley, CA: Digital Diner Press).

Lange, P. (2007) 'Publicly Private and Privately Public: Social Networking on YouTube', *Journal of Computer-Mediated Communication*, 13(1), 361–80.

Lazarsfeld, P. F. (1941) 'Remarks on Administrative and Critical Communications Research', *Studies in Philosophy and Social Science*, 9(1), 2–16.

Liebes, T. and Katz, E. (1990) *The Export of Meaning: Cross-Cultural Readings of Dallas* (Oxford: Oxford University Press).

Lievrouw, L. (2009) 'New Media, Mediation, and Communication Study', *Information, Communication & Society*, 12(3), 303–25.

Lievrouw, L. and Livingstone, S. (2002) 'Editorial Introduction', in L. Lievrouw and S. Livingstone (Eds) *Handbook of New Media: Social Shaping and Social Consequences of ICTs* (London: Sage Publications), 1–15.

Lister, M., Dovey, J., Giddings, S., Grant, I., Kelly, K. (2003) *New Media: A Critical Introduction* (London: Routledge).

Livingstone, S. (2009) 'On the Mediation of Everything: ICA Presidential Address 2008', *Journal of Communication*, 59(1), 1–18.

Livingstone, S. (2008) 'Taking Risky Opportunities in Youthful Content Creation: Teenagers' Use of Social Networking Sites for Intimacy, Privacy and Self-Expression', *New Media and Society*, 10(3), 393–411.

Livingstone, S. (Ed.) (2005a) *Audiences and Publics: When Cultural Engagement Matters for the Public Sphere* (Bristol: Intellect).

Livingstone, S. (2005b) 'On the Relation Between Audiences and Publics', in S. Livingstone (Ed.) *Audiences and Publics: When Cultural Engagement Matters for the Public Sphere* (Bristol: Intellect), 17–44.

Livingstone, S. (2004) 'The Challenge of Changing Audiences: Or, What Is the Audience Researcher to do in the Internet Age?', *European Journal of Communication*, 19(1), 75–86.

Livingstone, S. (1998) 'Relationships Between Media and Audiences: Prospects for Audience Reception Studies', in J. Curran and T. Liebes (Eds) *Media, Ritual and Identity* (London: Routledge).

Livingstone, S. (1994) 'The Rise and Fall of Audience Research: An Old Story with a New Ending', in M. R. Levy and M. Gurevitch (Eds) *Defining Media Studies: Reflections on the Future of the Field* (New York: Oxford University Press), 247–54.

Livingstone, S. and Lunt, P. (1994) *Talk on Television: Audience Participation and Public Debate* (London: Routledge).

Livingstone, S. and Thumim, N. (2003) *Assessing the Media Literacy of UK Adults: A Review of the Academic Literature*, Report commissioned by the Broadcasting Standards Commission/Independent Television Commission/British Film Institute/National Institute of Adult and Continuing Education.

Livingstone, S., Van Couvering, E. and Thumim, N. (2008) 'Converging Traditions of Research on Media and Information Literacies: Disciplinary, Critical and Methodological Issues', in J. Coiro, M. Knobel, C. Lankshear and D. J. Leu (Eds) *Handbook of Research on New Literacies* (New York and London: Lawrence Erlbaum Associates).

Livingstone, S., Van Couvering, E. and Thumim, N. (2005) *Adult Media Literacy: A Review of the Research Literature*, Report commissioned by The Office of Communications (Ofcom).

MacDonald, M. (2003) *Exploring Media Discourse* (London: Arnold Publishers).

Macdonald, S. (1996) 'Introduction', in S. Macdonald and G. Fyfe (Eds) *Theorizing Museums* (Oxford and Cambridge, MA: Blackwell Publishers).

Martin-Barbero, J. (1993) *Communication, Culture and Hegemony: From the Media to Mediations* (E. Fox and R. A. White, Trans.) (London: Sage Publications).

Marx, L. (1964) *The Machine in the Garden: Technology and the Pastoral Ideal in America* (New York: Oxford University Press).

Mast, J. (2009) 'New Directions in Hybrid Popular Television: A Reassessment of Television Mock-Documentary', *Media, Culture and Society*, 31(2), 231–50.

Mayo, M. (2006) 'Building Heavens, Havens or Hells? Community as Policy in the Context of the Post-Washington Consensus', in S. Herbrechter and M. Higgins (Eds) *Returning (to) Communities: Theory, Culture and Political Practice of the Communal* (New York and Amsterdam: Rodopi), 387–400.

McLean, F. (1997) *Marketing the Museum* (London: Routledge).

McRobbie, A. (2009) *The Aftermath of Feminism: Gender, Culture and Social Change* (London: Sage Publications).

Meadows, D. (2011) 'Photobus Website "Digital Storytelling"', http://www.photobus.co.uk/?id=534, retrieved 15 May 2011.

Meadows, D. (2003) 'Digital Storytelling: Research-Based Practice in New Media', *Visual Communication*, 2(2), 189–93.

Meadows, D. and Kidd, J. (2009) 'Capture Wales, The BBC Digital Storytelling Project', in J. Hartley and K. McWilliam (Eds) *Story Circle: Digital Storytelling around the World* (Oxford: Wiley-Blackwell).

Mehl, D (2005) 'The Public on the Television Screen: Towards a Public Sphere of Exhibition', in S. Livingstone (Ed.) *Audiences and Publics: When Cultural Engagement Matters for the Public Sphere* (Bristol and Portland, OR: Intellect Books).

Merrin, W. (2008) 'Media Studies 2.0 – My thoughts', 4 January, http://mediastudies2point0.blogspot.com/, retrieved 15 June 2011.

Message, K. and Healy, C. (2004) 'A Symptomatic Museum: The New, the NMA and the Culture Wars', *Borderlands E-Journal*, 3(3), 1–11.

Morley, D. (2009) 'Mediated Class-ifications: Representations of Class and Culture in Contemporary British Television', *European Journal of Cultural Studies*, 12(4), 487–508.

Morley, D. (2006) 'Unanswered Questions in Audience Research', *The Communication Review*, 9, 101–21.

Morley, D. (1980) *The Nationwide Audience: Structure and Decoding* (London: BFI).

Mosco, V. (2005) *The Digital Sublime: Myth, Power and Cyberspace* (Cambridge, MA and London: The MIT Press).

Mouffe, C. (2005) *On the Political: Thinking in Action* (New York: Routledge).

Mouffe, C. (1999) 'Deliberative Democracy or Agonistic Pluralism?', *Social Research*, 66(3), 746–58.

Murdock, G. (2010) 'Networking the Commons: Convergence Culture and the Public Interest' in Gripsrud, J. (Ed.) *Relocating Television: Television in the Digital Context* (Oxon: Routledge).

Murdock, G. (2000) 'Money Talks: Broadcasting Finance and Public Culture', in E. Buscombe (Ed.) *British Television: A Reader* (Oxford: Oxford University Press) 118–41.

Murdock, G. (1999) 'Rights and Representations: Public Discourse and Cultural Citizenship', in J. Gripsrud (Ed.) *Television and Common Knowledge* (London: Routledge).

Museum of London (2002) *Community Access Strategy 2002–2005* (Museum of London: Internal Document July 2002).

Museum of London Voices Exhibition November 2001–May 2002 (2002) 'Exit Interviews' from the Museum's, *Summative Evaluation* (Museum of London: Internal Document).

Neale, S. (Ed.) (2002) *Genre and Contemporary Hollywood* (London: BFI Publishing).

Neale, S. (2000) *Genre and Hollywood* (London: Routledge).

Negra, D. (2009) *What a Girl Wants? Fantasizing the Reclamation of Self in Postfeminism* (London and New York: Routledge).

Nintendo website, http://www.nintendo.co.uk/NOE/en_GB/news/tell-us-your-story.html#/Home/, retrieved 8 July 2011.

Nye, D. E. (1992) *Electrifying America: Social Meanings of a New Technology, 1880–1940* (Massachusetts: MIT Press).

O'Connell, R (2001) 'Heritage Lottery Fund, Revenue Grants Programme, Application Form: Museum of London'.

OFCOM (2010) 'The Communications Market 2010', http://stakeholders. ofcom.org.uk/market-data-research/market-data/communications-market-reports/cmr10/uk/, retrieved 6 May 2011.

Oral History Society Annual Conference (2004) http://www.oralhistory.org. uk/conferences/confdocs/2004.pdf, retrieved January 2005.

Palmer, G. (2002) 'Big Brother: An Experiment in Governance', *Television and New Media*, 3(3), 295–310.

Perkins, T. (2000) 'Who (and What) Is It for?', in C. Gledhill and L. Williams (Eds) *Reinventing Film Studies* (London: Arnold).

Pervasive Media Studio Website (2011) http://www.pmstudio.co.uk/what-pervasive-media, retrieved 12 July 2011.

Peters, J. D. (1999) *Speaking into the Air: A History of the Idea of Communication* (Chicago: University of Chicago Press).

Peters, J. D. (1993) 'Distrust of Representation: Habermas on the Public Sphere', *Media, Culture and Society*, 15(4), 541–71.

Piper, H. (2004) 'Reality TV, Wife Swap and the Drama of Banality', *Screen*, 45(4), 273–86.

Plummer, K. (2001) *Documents of Life 2: An Invitation to a Critical Humanism* (London: Sage Publications).

Pratt, M. L. (1981) 'The Short Story: The Long and the Short of It', *Poetics*, 10, 175–94.

Prosler, M. (1996) 'Museums and Globalisation', in S. Macdonald and G. Fyfe (Eds) *Theorizing Museums* (Oxford and Cambridge, MA: Blackwell).

Putnam, R. D. (2000) *Bowling Alone: The Collapse and Revival of American Community* (London: Simon & Schuster).

Raboy, M. (2008) 'Dreaming in Technicolor: The Future of PSB in a World Beyond Broadcasting', *Convergence: The International Journal of Research into New Media Technologies*, 14(3), 361–5.

Radway, J.(1984) *Reading the Romance: Women, Patriarchy and Popular Literature* (New York: Verso).

Renov, M. (2004) *The Subject of Documentary* (Minneapolis and London: University of Minnesota Press).

Rheingold, H. (1993) *The Virtual Community: Homesteading on the Electronic Frontier* (Reading, MA: Addison-Wesley).

Richards, E. (2011) 'Oxford Media Convention Speech 24 January', http://media.ofcom.org.uk/2011/01/24/oxford-media-convention-speech-by-ed-richards/, retrieved 6 May 2011.

Rose, N. (2001) 'Community, Citizenship and the Third Way', in D. Meredyth and J. Minson (Eds.) *Citizenship and Cultural Policy* (London and Thousand Oaks, CA and New Dehli: Sage Publications) 1–17.

Rosen, J. (2006) 'The People Formerly Known as the Audience', *Pressthink: Ghost of Democracy in the Media Machine*, 27 June, http://archive.pressthink.org/2006/06/27/ppl_frmr.html, retrieved 26 October 2011.

Ross, C. and Swain, H. (2001) *Museum of London: 25 Years 1976–2001* (Brochure) (London: Museum of London).

Sacks, H. (1984) 'On Doing Being Ordinary', in M. Atkinson and J. Heritage (Eds) *Structures of Social Action: Studies in Conversation Analysis* (Cambridge: Cambridge University Press).

Savage, M., Bagnall, G. and Longhurst, B. (2001) 'Ordinary, Ambivalent and Defensive: Class Identities in the Northwest of England', *Sociology*, 35(4), 875–92.

Scannell, P. (2000) 'For Anyone-as-Someone Structures', *Media, Culture and Society*, 22(1), 5–24.

Scannell, P. (1996a) 'Britain: Public Service Broadcasting, from National Culture to Multiculturalism', in M. Raboy (Ed.) *Public Broadcasting for the 21st Century* (Acamedia Research Monograph) (Luton: University of Luton Press).

Scannell, P. (1996b) *Radio, Television and Modern Life* (Oxford and Cambridge, MA: Blackwell).

Scannell, P. and Cardiff, D. (1991) *A Social History of British Broadcasting: Volume One, 1922–1939* (London: Basil Blackwell).

Schegloff, E. (1999) 'Schegloff's Texts' as "Billig's Data": A Critical Reply', *Discourse & Society*, 10, 558–72.

Schubert, C. (2000) *The Curator's Egg: The Evolution of the Museum Concept from the French Revolution to the Present Day* (London: One-Off Press).

Seaman, W. (1992) 'Active Audience Theory: Pointless Populism?', *Media, Culture and Society*, 14, 301–11.

Selwyn, N. (2003) 'Apart from Technology: Understanding People's Non-Use of Information and Communication Technologies in Everyday Life', *Technology in Society*, 25, 99–116.

Silver, D. (2004) 'Internet/Cyberculture/Digital Culture/New Media/Fill-in-the-Blank Studies', *New Media and Society*, 6(1), 55–64.

Silverstone, R. (2007) *The Media and Morality: On the Rise of the Mediapolis* (Cambridge and Malden, MA: Polity Press).

Silverstone, R. (2005) 'The Sociology of Mediation and Communication', in C. Calhoun, C. Rojek and B. Turner (Eds) *The SAGE Handbook of Sociology* (London: Sage Publications).

Silverstone, R. (1999) *Why Study the Media?* (London and Thousand Oaks, CA and New Delhi: Sage Publications).
Silverstone, R. (1994) *Television and Everyday Life* (London: Routledge).
Silverstone, R. and Hirsch E. (Eds) *Consuming Technologies: Media and Information in Domestic Spaces* (London: Routledge), 15–31.
Skeggs, B. (2009) 'Moral Economy of Person Production: The Class Relations of Self-Performance on "Reality" Television', *Sociological Review*, 57(4), 626–44.
Skeggs, B. (2004) *Class, Self, Culture* (London: Routledge).
Skeggs, B., Thumim, N. and Wood, H. (2008) ' "Oh Goodness, I Am Watching Reality TV": How Methods Make Class in Multi-Method Audience Research', *European Journal of Cultural Studies*, 11(1), 5–24.
Smith, A. (Ed.) (1974) *British Broadcasting* (Newton Abbot: David and Charles Holdings Ltd).
Smithsonian 1930s Family Day (2009) ' "Remembering the 1930s Family Day" and Recording of Oral Histories', *Media Advisory*, http://americanart.si.edu/pr/advisories/1930s_family_day_advisory.pdf, retrieved 1 May 2009.
Smithsonian About (2009) 'About the Art Museum and the Renwick Gallery', http://americanart.si.edu/visit/about/, retrieved 24 September 2009.
Smithsonian Strategic Plan (2009) http://www.si.edu/about/documents/SI_Strategic_Plan_Exec_Summary.pdf, retrieved 24 September 2009.
Sola, T. (1992) 'Museum Professionals: The Endangered Species', in P. Boylan (Ed.) *Museums 2000: Politics, People, Professionals and Profits* (New York: Routledge).
Sussman, G. (2003) 'Introduction: The Struggle for and within Public Television', *Television and New Media*, 4(2), 111–15.
Tarrow, S. (2005) *The New Transnational Activism* (Cambridge: Cambridge University Press).
Telegraph (2011) 'One in Nine People Now Have a Facebook Account', http://www.telegraph.co.uk/technology/facebook/8621513/One-in-nine-has-a-Facebook-account-worldwide.html, retrieved 12 July 2011.
Thompson, J. B. (1995) *The Media and Modernity: A Social Theory of the Media* (Cambridge: Polity).
Thompson, P. (2000) *The Voice of the Past: Oral History*, 3rd edn. (New York: Oxford University Press).
Thumim, N. (2010) 'Self-Representation in Museums: Therapy or Democracy? in Self-Mediation: Citizenship and New Media', *Critical Discourse Studies* 7(3), Special Issue, 291–304.
Thumim, N. (2009a) 'Exploring Self-Representations in Wales and London: Tension in the Text', in J. Hartley and K. McWilliam (Eds.) *Story Circle: Digital Storytelling Around the World* (Oxford: Wiley-Blackwell).
Thumim, N. (2009b) ' "Everyone Has a Story to Tell": Mediation and Self Representation in two UK Institutions', *International Journal of Cultural Studies*, 12(6), 617–38.
Thumim, N. (2008) ' "It's Good for Them to Know My Story": Cultural Mediation as Tension', in K. Lundby (Ed.) *Digital Storytelling, Mediatized Stories: Self-Representations in New Media* (New York: Peter Lang Publishing).

Thumim, N. (2007) *Mediating Self-Representations: Tensions Surrounding 'Ordinary' Participation in Public Sector Projects*, Unpublished PhD thesis, LSE, University of London.

Thumim, N. (2006) 'Mediated Self-Representations: "Ordinary People" in "Communities" ', in S. Herbrechter and M. Higgins (Eds.) *Returning (to) Communities: Theory, Culture and Political Practice of the Communal* (Amsterdam, Netherlands and New York: Rodopi B. V.).

Turkle, S. (1997) *Life on the Screen: Identity in the Age of the Internet* (New York: Touchstone).

Turner, G. (2010) *Ordinary People and the Media: The Demotic Turn* (London: Sage Publications).

Turner, G. (2004) *Understanding Celebrity* (London: Sage Publications).

Urry, J. (1996) 'How Societies Remember the Past', in S. Macdonald and G. Fyfe (Eds) *Theorizing Museums* (Oxford and Cambridge, MA: Blackwell).

Van Zoonen, L. (2001) 'Desire and Resistance: Big Brother and the Recognition of Everyday Life', *Media, Culture and Society*, 23(5), 667–9.

Walsh, K. (1992) *The Representation of the Past: Museums and Heritage in the Post Modern World* (London and New York: Routledge).

Wardle, C. and Williams, A. (2010) 'Beyond User-Generated Content: A Production Study Examining the Ways in Which UGC Is Used at the BBC', *Media Culture & Society*, 32(5), 781–99.

Wardle, C. and Williams, A. (2008) 'ugc@thebbc: Understanding Its Impact upon Contributors, Non-Contributors and BBC News' (Cardiff: Cardiff School of Journalism Media and Cultural Studies, University of Cardiff/BBC/AHRC), http://www.cardiff.ac.uk/jomec/resources/UserGeneratedContent_ClaireWardle.pdf , retrieved 15 June 2011.

Williams, R. (2002 [1958]) 'Culture is Ordinary', in B. Highmore (Ed.) *The Everyday Life Reader* (London and New York: Routledge).

Williams, R. (1983) *Keywords: A Vocabulary of Culture and Society*, 2nd edn. (London: Fontana Press).

Williams, R. (1978) 'Utopia and Science Fiction', *Science Fiction Studies*, 5(3), 203–14.

Williams, R. (1977) 'From Reflection to Mediation', in R. Williams (Ed.) *Marxism and Literature* (Oxford: Oxford University Press).

Williamson, J. (1993) 'Democracy and the "Washington Consensus" ', *World Development*, 21(8), 1329–36.

Wilson, P. and Stewart, M. (2008a) *Global Indigenous Media: Cultures, Poetics and Politics* (Durham and London: Duke University Press).

Wilson, P. and Stewart, M. (2008b) 'Introduction: Indigeneity and Indigenous Media on the Global Stage', in P. Wilson and M. Stewart (Eds.) *Global Indigenous Media: Cultures, Poetics and Politics* (Durham and London: Duke University Press), 1–35.

Witcomb, A. (2003) *Re-Imagining the Museum: Beyond the Mausoleum* (London: Routledge).

Wright, W. (1975) *Six Guns and Society: A Structural Study of the Western* (Berkeley, CA: University of California Press).

Yee, N. and Bailenson, J. (2007) 'The Proteus Effect: The Effect of Transformed Self-Representation on Behavior', *Human Communication Research*, 33(3), 271–90.

Index